Burning Down the Fireproof Hotel

*an invitation to
the beautiful life*

Lee,
I have loved getting to know you,
calling you friend.
Keep "burning brightly" finding

Cary Campbell Umhau

all life and God's best for you—
Cary

All scripture quotations are taken from The Holy Bible, New International Version®, NIV®. Copyright © 1973, 1978, 1984 by Biblica, Inc.® Used by permission. All rights reserved worldwide.

Hands of Time ("Brian's Song")
Written by Alan Bergman, Marilyn Bergman, & Michel Legrand
© 1972 Colgems – EMI Music Inc. All rights administered by Sony/ATV Music Publishing LLC., Suite 1200, 424 Church Street, Nashville, TN 37219. All rights reserved. Used by permission.

Glorious Day (Living He Loved Me)
Written by John Mark Hall and Michael Bleecker
© 2009 Sony/ATV Music Publishing LLC, Word Music and My Refuge Music. All rights on behalf of Sony/ATV Music Publishing LLC administered by Sony/ATV Music Publishing LLC, 424 Church Street, Suite 1200, Nashville, TN 37219. All rights reserved. Used by permission.

Copyright © 2009 My Refuge Music (BMI) (adm. at CapitolCMGPublishing. com)/Word Music (ASCAP)/Sony/ATV Tree Pub (BMI). All rights reserved. Used by permission.

© 2009 Word Music LLC, Club Zoo Music, SWECS Music. All rights reserved. Used by permission.

Wide Open Spaces
Words and Music by Susan Gibson
© 1997 PIE EYED GROOBEE MUSIC. All rights administered by BUG MUSIC, INC., a BMG/CHYRSALIS COMPANY). All Rights Reserved. Used by Permission. Reprinted by Permission of Hal Leonard Corporation

ISBN: 978-0-9863002-0-2

Cover art, book design, editing: Ben Kolesar (www.onepagebible.net)

This book is for all you people, friends and strangers, about whom I find myself blurting out to God, "You outdid yourself when you made *this one!*"

Lila, Carter, and Charlie, wanting to lead you into freedom made me fight to breathe fresh air when I could have been tempted to stay in the asbestos.

Andrew, when I first met you – in a mud puddle no less – you asked, "Do you want me to carry you?" And carry me you have. Thanks for being the *someone* who's watched over me. The best is yet to come.

Set me on fire with love for you, God.

My own dangerous prayer

He brought me out into a spacious place.
He rescued me because he delighted in me.

Psalm 18:19

I have need to be all on fire
for I have mountains of ice around me to melt.

William Lloyd Garrison

MANY YEARS AGO, when I was a young mother, on a summer day with perfect weather, in a charming beach town where my family and I had gone to enjoy the surf and sun, I realized that I wanted to run away.

I pulled into a gas station with a movie-star-handsome husband who loved and took good care of me, three cute, healthy children, enough money to refuel our monster gas-guzzler and what should have been hints of an existential crisis.

In those days before pay-at-the-pump, I walked into the Mini-Mart wielding our VISA card while my husband did the dirty work of pumping the gas.

As I approached the cash register, time stood still. I remember the glare of harsh fluorescent lights as I froze and stared at the racks of Cheetos and pork rinds and the vials of strange caffeine products that guarantee that long-haul truckers won't nod off before they get their loads to Reno.

I can still hear the piped-in, elevator music version of *Brian's Song*, a tearjerker from the Seventies about a cancer-stricken football player ("If the hands of time were hands that I could hold ...").

I saw the dingy tiled floor rising up to meet me, and the air-freshener rack looked like a Tilt-a-Whirl coming at me as the room – and I – spun a little.

I realized that I wanted to run down the hall beyond the bathrooms, just past the bucket full of green cleaning solution with a grimy mop protruding from it, out the back exit beyond the dumpsters. I'd just keep going across that barren South Carolina field of dry grass blanched by the summer sun, strewn with cigarette butts and broken beer bottles, and I'd run forever.

I wanted to escape my beautiful life.

I hadn't known it before that moment, but all of a sudden I knew it with complete certainty.

And instead of running I signed the gas chit and slowly walked out the way I'd come in, through the glass doors with those vertical stickers on them that help the clerk determine the height of the bad guys storming out with wads of stolen cash.

My 5 foot, 3 inch self marched back to our blue Suburban, hoisted myself up to the shotgun position, turned and cheerily said something or other to my waiting clan, and we wheeled away to more family fun, probably another trip to the Dipper Dan ice cream parlor.

And I shoved down that message from the universe that

told me I was not enjoying this vacation – or my happy Christian life – quite as much as I thought I was.

* * *

Twenty years later, I live with the same husband in the same house on the same street in Washington D.C. And yet everything is different.

This is a story of escaping "the good life" and finding my own life – a life that's bigger, scarier, and more beautiful than anything I could have planned.

I'm nobody special.

But I do happen to be one of God's favorites.

The fact is … you are too.

We don't usually believe that, do we?

For a long time I lived like I was in a fireproof building, avoiding God's blazing love for me. I wasn't taking advantage of my birthright – encounters with a laughing Jesus and feasts at a big old banquet table with a bunch of good people.

I was missing my own life.

Until God asked me something akin to "Where are you?"

I saw that I was hiding from him, holed up in a way of life that kept me from truly living, in a structure tainted with asbestos.

God chose to woo me out, call me forth, and urge me to step out ever so gingerly. Over the course of a long, hard decade or so, he showed me my own pain and defenses and pointed out where *he* was – with me.

He did it through people, through kindness, through invitation, and mostly by disrupting my neatly laid plans.

What follows is an unorthodox memoir of the journey from fear and shame to the freedom that comes from knowing that I am seen, known, and loved just as I am – wobbly, vulnerable, rarely cool, and also, as it turns out, worth knowing.

This is a jumble of stories – part of one big story – about moving from loneliness to belonging, from perfunctory participation in Christian culture to a deep, sustaining faith that God is who he says he is and that he is more than enough.

What these stories have in common is that each one showed me more of God. Each showed me something about him that I had hoped was true but hadn't much believed despite growing up in church.

Eventually I came to believe that my life has deep meaning, great purpose, and much adventure ahead.

There's a kingdom awaiting, one that is about invitation and not punishment, power and not lip service, laughter and not legalism. It's a love-fest journey with a custom-made, crazy quilt family to which we already belong. God's perfect order will be restored, not to mind-numbingly boring clouds and harps but to all that was intended, to this earth made whole, your people without tears, no more sorrow, all joy.

You may be wondering where that promised life is, where you'll find the good life. I sure wondered. The quest I've been on may be your quest too. My story will only be valuable to you if it piques your interest in finding the love that's out there for the taking, the spacious life that's available to God's favorites.

The fact is ... that's all of us.

Come on. Are you in?

It won't be the same without you.

I thought God wanted cookie-cutter Christians. Now I know he's got more than one mold (and they're flexible).

"The glory of God is a human being fully alive," the second-century bishop Irenaeus once said.

I used to think God was looking for respectable people – those who didn't mix with the wrong crowd, folks whose desires were never too strong, who recognized Jesus as good but weren't going to get all radical about him. The men simply needed to stay sober, make a lot of money, and drive their wives and kids to church in large vehicles with those window stickers depicting the perfect family. The women would put hearts and bows on everything, keep their opinions to themselves, and certainly never travel alone. The children would stay on the college prep path and never deviate.

And even though I wanted parts of that life, I worried that if I became an all-in, committed Jesus girl I'd stop being *me*. I'd develop a taste for cheesy art – garden gates and dreamy paths – and have to give up my taste for Howard Finster and Matisse. I'd lose my appetite for margaritas and start craving watered-down, churchy-pink punch. I'd have to leave urban streets for a quiet convent even though I'm kind of scared of nuns.

Instead I found out that the longer we hang out with God and the more we gulp in his love, the more we become ourselves, our own versions of God's image. It still shocks me that he allows us to represent him. It doesn't seem wise.

Although I appear confident, I'm often a fragile mess. I love driving in fast-moving traffic and I hear God best on the road. I rescue random handicrafts from thrift stores because I feel sad for whoever made them. I'm probably the only debutante who ever sent her photos to Leavenworth Prison, to a pen pal who shellacked them onto plaques, burnished the edges, and sent them back. And I have a great imagination, which means that whenever anyone I love is late, I immediately assume they've been chopped into pieces. God can work with that package.

As I've grown into my set-free self, I've started to look more and more like the kid I was on my better days. I resemble the girl who took just about any dare, getting stuck in a chimney once, and had imaginary playmates – Mrs. Sivvers, Grock, The Berber, Mother Evilly and another crew, always a unit, named Peter-Wendy-Allen-and-the-baby – all of whose exploits I loved to share.

If God has wooed me with a quirky approach, it may be because "quirky" was my native tongue.

My paternal grandfather was a record-breaking aviator, an oil wildcatter, a novelist, and a rogue. He married a former Mardi Gras queen who largely supported him and who ended each and every day by going to bed with a shot of bourbon, a glass of warm beer and a cup of black coffee. Their son, my father, was prone to hiring midgets for campaigns in the early, heady days of advertising. He had his last drink in 1957, plays the ukulele, and never stopped noticing struggling people even as he soared to the upper echelons of the Thoroughbred horseracing world, winning the Preakness and the Belmont, two legs of the famed Triple Crown.

When I was 11 and was being bullied by a crowd of older girls at the barn where I kept my pony, I confided in my father, knowing that he had the wisdom to know how I should react. He told me, "Next time they bother you, just wheel around and say to them, 'Go to hell, bitches!'" I did exactly that; the teasing stopped.

My mother came from a well-respected line of Baptist preachers and lived her early years in a grand antebellum Georgia home that General Sherman missed. She had a schizophrenic uncle whom her mother insisted was normal. She has taught Sunday school and Bible studies most of her life, smoked cigars for a while, and recently tap-danced to *It's Raining Men* for her great-grandchildren.

One of my earliest memories involves my maternal grandmother taking me to see the movie *Hell's Angels on Wheels*. I felt exhilarated in the cozy dark seated with my sister, young cousins, and our very proper matriarch with grey curls, church-worthy dress, and high heels in the midst of a crew of black-leather-chapped, muscle-bound motorcycle enthusiasts, watching a movie that was, I now realize, entirely inappropriate for our merry little crew.

When I think of myself as most fully alive, I remember being a teenager enraptured by a perfect day of 68 degrees or so. I picked sprigs and stalks of the azaleas that bloomed profusely in my hometown of Atlanta, Georgia each spring and tucked them behind my ears, in my buttonholes, and in the belt loops of my jeans. I twirled and danced around in circles, dizzy with the joy of being alive ... until a boy that I liked drove by and honked, and I darted into the side door of the house and put twirling on hold for a few decades.

In my bedroom aerie, with the roar of the air-conditioner as my soundtrack, I would spend hours reading and writing in my journal. I'd stare down at my parents and sister sun-tanning in the backyard and wonder why I was different, the white sheep in a bronzed family.

At summer camp when other teenagers were competing for sports trophies, I won Fastest Typist. It wasn't that I was a sedentary introvert. I was simply over-awed by all the cool girls who made everything look easy and thought I'd sit out a few rounds. I was also dodging wearing a bathing suit, in which I felt shamefully pale and overweight, even at 100 pounds.

I was the sports mascot in high school, accompanying the cheerleaders and bouncing around in purple high-tops and a fake-fur, full-body suit covered in leopard spots, even though we were the Northside Tigers. My mother hadn't been able to find tiger fur at the store, so we improvised.

Nonplussed, I danced, frolicked, and even twirled on the gravelly sidelines of our Friday night football games. The smell of hot dogs and Coke wafted through the air as the marching band played *Dancing Queen*, *Shake Your Booty*, and *The Hustle* (the last one seemingly over and over). Boys teased me and children pulled my tail. With giddy joy welling up behind that white fake-fur tiger tummy, I felt bold and free as long as I had on my mask.

Life with Jesus seemed rather abstract until I stole the baby powder.

My official God-and-Jesus story started with a class B misdemeanor. In Sunday school, I'd heard about Jesus feeding people with loaves and fish and walking on water and all, but I hadn't known faith had anything to do with shoplifting and sleepovers and forgiveness. And me.

Navigating as I was the uneven terrain of Southern girlhood and middle school, when I was 13 I started slipping away from home to tiptoe on the wild side. Many afternoons I'd jump on the 23/Oglethorpe bus with my neatly braided, auburn hair and tasteful clothes, ride up Peachtree Street through Buckhead, and select a store to honor with a visit. I would then shoplift a few things and get back home in time to watch *Petticoat Junction* with our maid Mattie before dutifully doing my *Wordly Wise* vocabulary homework and my algebra.

One day I marched into a Sears store, stole a container of Love's Baby Soft Powder, and was promptly apprehended by the store detective. He didn't know that I'd already been stealing bags-full of other items from a number of fine establishments for well over a year (including – if I do say so – a rather impressive haul of 17 record albums at one time, Jethro Tull's *Aqualung* and Cat Stevens' *Tea for the Tillerman* probably still my favorites in the lot).

After dragging in my parents, the detective released me, a puny fish not worth the hassle of further processing.

Rather than skewer me because I was now a criminal, my mother had a surprising reaction. She said some things about Jesus forgiving me and how she also forgave me; she said that I could still go to my friend Julie's sleepover that night.

I could have (maybe) believed that God loved me on the days when I sang beatifically, if a bit off-key, in the church choir and did all my chores. It blew me away to hear that God loved me even if Sears was going to hang a wanted poster with my young teenaged face on it in their employee lounge, probably for perpetuity.

I wanted in.

More or less unceremoniously I decided to take up with this Jesus.

I used to try to memorize lines so I could act my part. Then I spilled coffee on my script and couldn't read it anymore.

For years after my shoplifting conversion, I was God's press agent, even speaking at church and on the radio about what it was like to be a model Christian teenager.

I figured I was living pretty darn well, better than most everyone else at least, and I thought that if I did my part, God would do his. Ironically I thought my part was far more about following rules than about following Jesus. For a couple of decades afterwards, life was dictated by a set of unquestionable principles and commensurate guarantees:

»   People will like you if you can read their minds and meet their expectations.
»   Once you seal the deal and get married, all the lonely longings will end.
»   If you follow all of life's rules, you will be safe and untouchable.
»   Cancer is for other people.
»   Being white, Christian, and American makes you special.
»   Make sure you're a perfect mother or your children will have sex and get tattoos.
»   If you screw up or even look like you don't have it all together, you'll ruin your "witness," which means other people won't find Jesus, which means you will have helped consign them to hell.

» If you're vulnerable and wobbly, people will avoid you.
» God wants, above all else, for you to be happy, and if you're not, you're doing something wrong.

Oh the expectations were endless – and they changed depending upon which subculture I spent the day in. I had to live in a mansion on the right street with important antique pieces to impress neighbors, and yet when friends who lived in other parts of town stopped by my house, I also had to have enough funky art and a certain studied look of neglect to prove to them that I wasn't the materialistic sort.

I tried to impress some friends with stories of my vacations to esoteric places. Then with other people, I needed to downplay the expensive trips and emphasize how much money I gave away to politically correct charities and Christian causes.

I had to be thin and fit in spite of the fact that mayonnaise and salt were my favorite foods and that I'd been raised down South, where people often feel slighted if you refuse wedges of their homemade pound cake.

Church attendance was required but I shouldn't bother going if I was having a bad day (which I often was) because it was critical to be happy-clappy in church.

I got married and had children early, which saved me from sorting out what I should do with my life. That was fortunate, since I'd had no career goals other than driving the Oscar Mayer Wienermobile around the country (an aspiration that had more to do with running away from my impossible expectations of myself than it did with a love of hot dogs).

With my rules intact, I assumed our family would breeze through life and impress people. We'd make friends and join the right groups, clubs, and church. Sitting in that church together, I assumed we were being collectively admired for some vague virtue by people I alternately feared and tried to impress.

I had long gone through life trying to attract the right sorts of people and avoid the wrong sorts, the ones I assumed God didn't much like, the ones my big-hearted sister included in the social forays that I skipped. I'd be poisoned or something if I got near them – like inhaling so much secondhand smoke.

Here is an incomplete list of the sorts of people I have disdained or mistrusted in my life (so far):

> » Those who are uneducated or who have bad grammar
> » Anyone not white
> » The mentally ill
> » Gay people
> » People who use the f-word
> » Democrats

- » Republicans
- » The poor
- » The rich
- » Those who don't act or think quickly
- » The impulsive
- » The conventional
- » People who don't care what others think
- » The fearful who seek safety above all
- » Non-Christians
- » Christians
- » Myself

I once read about a Thai woman who got lost when she took the wrong bus, ended up crossing the border to Malaysia, and could not explain to anyone what had happened, since she spoke only a local Malay dialect, Yawi. She lived on the streets and later in a shelter until health workers visiting the town 25 years after her disappearance heard her singing a song, recognized the dialect, and spoke with her. She was reunited with her family members who were – needless to say – quite shocked to see her again.

In many ways, as life progressed, I wondered if I too had climbed on the wrong bus and sped off on a life that somehow wasn't really mine to a place I didn't recognize.

How had I gotten there?

Where was I going next?

I used to think I was God's gift to other people. Now I realize I arrived at the friendship party late (without a hostess gift).

When I was a toddler just learning to talk, I spoke with a nasal tone. No one knew why until the day I sneezed and expelled a great volume of nasty matter from my nose – the chewed-up fingers and toes of my doll, Sassy, which I had anxiously bitten off and stuck up there. It seems that I'd long sought something to fill me – whether food, fiberfill, or friends.

As I settled into adulthood, in spite of being married with a full social calendar, I often felt lonely. I treated my acquaintances like projects and became obsessed with finding the one person on the planet that surely existed just to validate me and whose friendship would make me whole. I actually thought somebody could fill the pit in me that gaped and yawned and was waiting to be filled to overflowing.

Over about five years I ripped through two or three (okay, four) relationships that I weighed down with the burden of proving my worth to myself and to the world.

Smashing people into a mold that way doesn't turn out so well.

I finally came to the end of my efforts after burning out an important relationship in a vulnerable and visible way.

I then spent a long, long time home alone trying to avoid people and convinced that I wasn't fit for society and never would be. I slipped into a depression that didn't let go for a while.

I went through the motions with my husband and children, grateful for their needs which propelled me into normalcy much of the time. But many days when my family wasn't home, I stretched out on the living room floor, stared at the ashes in the fireplace, and detested myself for the depth of my longings to connect to people.

I dared God to come get me off the floor and set me back down in the little game of life if he wanted to bother.

And apparently he heard me and found me worth the trouble.

Life begins after some of the spinning plates hit the ground. So why do we work so hard to keep them all going?

In my experience, the message they preach in churches is often incomplete. They don't tell you that the way to joy is often through pain and that in the end the joy trumps the pain.

And shatters it.

And has the final word.

You only find that out through having your life fall apart, whether in increments, in big chunks or, as we say around my house to describe how much cake we want, in slivers, slices and slabs.

Disruption can ultimately be a gift ... like a building razed to make room for a better one.

Over time, God dismantled my safe house, my fireproof life. He did it by letting me see his presence and faithfulness, enough and more than enough, in the midst of relational disappointments, my own screw-ups, and hurts and betrayals I didn't think I could withstand ... you know, *life*.

The first intrusion was cancer. Well, sort of.

Statistically speaking, a lot of readers will have had horrific experiences with cancer. You've had your life flipped upside down by biopsies and chemo and fear. You've faced the brute, and it has stolen precious people from you after beastly battles. I hate cancer; I hate disease; I hate suffering. And I am genuinely and seriously sorry for yours in a way I wasn't able to be back in 1994 when I was 34 and I didn't even feel sad about my own breast cancer.

I had the best possible diagnosis if I had to have it at all, *intraductal carcinoma in situ*. I was cured with a mastectomy and nothing else. I don't even consider myself a proper, card-carrying cancer survivor. I cringe when someone thinks I'm part of the club, because I really didn't pay the dues and I don't want to mock another's suffering by equating mine. For a while it secretly embarrassed me that I had *cancer lite*, like I couldn't even do cancer well.

But cancer did give me an ironclad excuse when one of the elementary school room mothers telephoned me to see if I would bake brownies or cookies for Family Fun Day. I felt a sick sort of triumph as I breezily told her, "I'm sorry I can't help with the bake sale. I'm having my breast removed that day." Note to self: it's not normal when it's worth the price of a body part to have an excuse to finally say no to something.

A brush with cancer is generally a wake-up call, a chance to take stock of life and do all sorts of soul-searching and to reorient around an epiphany and *live as I always meant to live*. I missed that wake-up call, hitting snooze on an intended gift of perspective and growth, the opportunity to face mortality, admit my fears, and grieve the loss of a breast. I noted it as a blip on the radar screen, but I certainly didn't do business with God over it, afraid as I was to acknowledge pain or worry.

Cancer was another thing I tried to do perfectly, trying to inspire the many people who helped take care of my small children and made Rice Krispy Treats for us, folks whom I assumed were observing me like one might watch an after school special or a made-for-TV movie.

Within six weeks of my mastectomy, I was on the church speaking circuit as a newly minted wise person, giving galvanizing sermonettes on how to discover beauty in the ashes of life's tragedies.

I hope my words helped someone. They probably did, but only because people tend to hear what they need to hear in those sorts of messages, often in spite of us. After a talk, there's almost always a comment like, "The thing that you said about the trip to Utah was the most helpful part to me."

Which is nice and all, except that I've never been to Utah, and I feel quite sure I didn't say I had.

**

Oddly enough, a craft project gone wrong made a bigger impression than cancer had.

When my children were little, I decided to work some maternal magic and show them how to make gingerbread houses. Except I couldn't make the damn things work. The walls wouldn't adhere; the icing was too dry; the angles didn't hold. They were a failure. Which meant – didn't it? – that *I* was a failure.

My husband walked in the back door from work, oblivious to the unfolding drama as he entered my domestic domain of supposed mastery and proceeded to wow the little people by quickly assembling geodesic gingerbread domes. Okay, perhaps they were normal log cabins, foursquare and plain, but to me he worked wonders, he *was* a wonder, and – it somehow followed – I was a piece of crap and a worthless mother, and my children were the most pitiable creatures in all of the kingdom of childhood because of me. And furthermore that was obvious to everyone else.

"What sort of mother can't make gingerbread houses?" I wailed. "Christmas is ruined!" And I ran out of the room into hiding.

This neon sign saying that maybe I was a teensy-weensy bit fragile led me briefly to counseling, but I didn't stay for long or ask enough questions to begin finding relief.

It's a good day when all my plans come together perfectly. But riding around in tow trucks can be quite stellar too.

A few years later I was on a solo, month-long road trip around America. I'd stopped at a reunion of my college friends, the Wasabis, and I was going to be the first to leave California on the last day. I had a long day ahead of me. I knew from the map that I was going to be driving through a virtual roadside hospitality desert, and I wanted to get to a town where the motels had soap and locks on the door.

At 6 a.m. I tried to start Zippy. That's my six-speed MINI Cooper whom I've anthropomorphized and who has a guest book for people to sign, checkerboard side mirrors and, from my perspective at least, lots of personality.

Zippy had been fine the night before, but she wasn't co-operating with my plans for an early departure. It was cold and sleeting, and I called AAA – which I'd joined *just in case* – but I could only get cell reception if I angled my phone a certain way, which was difficult under an umbrella in the back-roads dark and wind.

As I waited to talk to the nice AAA lady who'd made sure I was safe before putting me on hold, I felt like God was saying, "I'm just as trustworthy today as I've been on the rest of this trip." We don't usually know what days are going to be about, but in a flash I knew that this day would provide a chance to grapple with whether God really *is* faithful and was still with me on the road trip even if it was shaping up to be a bit crappy.

Is a good day one in which whatever I had planned comes together just like I'd hoped it would? Or is a good day one in which whatever *should* happen *does* happen? I realized right then and there that I tend to think every day should go a certain way – my way. But really, days are parts of weeks, months, years, lives, and eternity, not distinct units that have to work according to my specifications.

Sometimes I hate that.

It's easy to see God in riotous wildflowers or in being forgiven for shoplifting, but it's harder to see him in the voice of the tow truck driver telling me that my car's battery is fine but that my car decidedly is not.

While the tow truck driver had been assessing the situation, my reunion friends had awakened. They were kindly scurrying to try to help me when one of them said something like, "We'll see what God does for you *now*," which hurt a little on my behalf and a lot on God's. She didn't really think God was showing up in her life much those days, and I stung with the realization that I'd probably sounded like some Christian bookmark all weekend, full of platitudes and easy answers to her life and to mine.

Jeff the tow truck driver got Zippy up on his big flatbed. After I collected all the coins and pens and tampons that had rolled under the cab in the sleety darkness when I dropped my purse, I hoisted myself up into the passenger seat next to him and off we went.

He turned out to be an awesome guy. He was 20 years old, probably 300 pounds, with red hair and soulful, brown eyes. We stopped right away at his friends' gas station where I treated us to Red Bull and doughnuts because he'd been up all night rescuing people like me, and I was ready for breakfast. He was really wise in helping me think through my options, which was great because I didn't really have many.

My rescuer decided we'd have to go all the way to Reno, and so we did, taking the long way through the mountains he loves so much so I could see his favorite spots bathed in the splendor of sunrise. He had me scratching my head and my preconceived notions about blue-collar workers as he regaled me with stories of his life and family, using one of the most extensive vocabularies I've encountered.

We left Zippy at a service bay that was closed on Sundays, shoving a note and a key through the night-drop slot. As I got organized to leave the car, the rain soaked my clothes when my umbrella inverted and blew away. That's when I saw the rainbow, all bright and encouraging. In that moment, I thought of a magnet a friend had once given me that had a Roger Miller quote on it, "Some people walk in the rain, others just get wet," and I tilted my face to the sky, trying to be worthy of that sentiment. I felt a little proud that I wasn't falling apart yet even though my car had.

Jeff waited patiently, which he didn't mind too much, us being best friends and all by then.

I asked him whether people mostly resigned themselves to their car disasters or whether they railed against them. He said, "It's 50-50, but it's cool when people realize that something even better might happen when their plans get interrupted."

I knew that was God's truth, and I had to talk around a lump in my throat when I said, "Yea, I never would have met you if this hadn't happened." Jeff grinned at me. I beamed back.

He drove me in search of a rental car and we parted, but not until I asked him if I could take a picture of us together. He remarked that a surprising number of people want to take such photos. I was tempted to feel less special to Jeff for a second but, still, we had a good enough goodbye with a fuzzy photo to prove it.

Within the hour I got involved in reporting a suspicious suitcase that had been left unattended near where I picked up my rental car. Then after I checked into my hotel to wait out a car repair that wouldn't start until morning at best, the police got called in to mediate a heated domestic dispute right outside my room, and I watched through the peephole with my pulse racing, wondering if the door was bulletproof and if they could hear me breathing.

Later I went out for dinner, and there was a roof leak over (only) my table.

I was talking to God a lot about what he had in mind and why Zippy and I weren't together even though I had really thought this road trip was a good idea, even a gift from God himself. That didn't necessarily guarantee, I realized now, that it would be a trouble-free day.

Or trip.

Or life.

The day ended with me naked and doubled over in hysterical laughter as I found out the hard way that some jokester who'd occupied the hotel room before me had apparently turned the showerhead into the bathroom itself, away from the confines of the fiberglass tub. In the same motion I had turned the water on to wait for it to heat up and pivoted to brush my teeth. So I hadn't noticed the water's wayward trajectory until it reached my feet and the carpet outside the door pretty much at the same time.

For much of my life I had been a woman standing on a beach watching occasional messages in a bottle float in with the tide. They said things like "You had enough allowance to buy the Jethro Tull album, you know," or "It was just a gingerbread house," or "Cancer is a legitimate reason to admit that life isn't perfect," or "Happy mothers would rather go get ice cream than disappear out the back door of the gas station," or "You're not loving your life as much as you insist you are."

I just thought that all the messages were addressed to someone else.

Until I couldn't mistake God's presence in the midst of the ultra-bizarro day that started in Jeff's tow-truck and ended with me naked and laughing in Reno.

And then I got a personal message in the form of a fireproof hotel.

I had a route mapped out. And it hadn't included Wheeling.

Wheeling, West Virginia had seen better days. There was a mobile home on wheels stuck in an intersection, but nobody much cared (I don't think they were going anywhere in a hurry). One business did both shoe repair and taxidermy, and *Light Up Your Life with Christ* was still strung up in Christmas lights in April, unlit and missing a few bulbs. The stripper bar and the Hostess Outlet shared a parking lot; you could get Twinkies and gawk at the girls without moving your car. It was a decent enough town, but probably one you had to know to love. Hardly the sort of place – if I were God – to which I'd direct anybody.

Minutes before I reached Wheeling, Zippy and I, reunited, had been zooming down Highway 70, and I had sensed a few miles out that Wheeling had something to say to me – or rather that God had something to say to me through Wheeling. Some people might consider it odd, but I was starting to get used to following whispers that I believed were from God. To try to tune in to the message I felt he had for me, I swerved off the road at that exit.

I cruised up and down what there was of a downtown, slowing down here and there, taking a few notes and wandering on again, more or less praying to be open to whatever God wanted to show me through this odd course correction.

When I came upon the Rogers Fireproof Hotel smack in

the middle of downtown, I inexplicably knew that it was the personal beacon I'd been seeking. I whipped Zippy over to the sidewalk, threw a nickel in the meter, trotted across the street, and started taking pictures of the substantial brick structure from every angle. I was looking for clues as to why I was standing in a strange town looking at an abandoned building. None were obvious.

When I arrived home to D.C. a few hours later, I researched it and discovered that in its heyday the Rogers Fireproof Hotel, built in 1914 and shuttered in the Nineties, had attracted many snazzy travelers for the annual Wheeling Jamboree country music festival. Many folks had, I surmised, enjoyed the roomy lobby, the inexplicably tropical-themed lounge, and – of course – the promise of sleeping fireproof.

For days as I thought about the now-dilapidated hotel's golden age, that tired town, and my own strange excursion there, I prayed to decode this enigmatic personal message from God.

Initially a fireproof hotel struck me as a pretty handy concept. My father happened to have burned down two boarding houses in West Virginia in his younger days, before he got a serious drinking problem under control and quit smoking in bed.

Yet as I thought more about my own half hour or so in Wheeling, I realized that fireproof might be good for *buildings*, but it wasn't right for my *life*.

I caught on to the fact that I was contemplating a visual metaphor for my own story. The sight of the Rogers Fireproof Hotel showed me, in retrospect, that I had long lived fireproof, holding life at bay.

And in a flash I could see that what I'd really wanted way back in that gas station in South Carolina, rather than escaping my beautiful life, was to begin to *inhabit* it.

But first I had needed to find out that fire wouldn't hurt me.

Actually the right sort of fire would save me.

In fact it had already begun to.

I thought love was all about Valentine's Day and romance. That's not necessarily where the action is.

Love showed up at the International Arrivals Terminal at Dulles Airport. I was waiting for a friend to arrive when I witnessed a reunion of two women, perhaps sisters, cousins or friends. They were both around 30. When one of them came through the door from Customs they came together in an embrace that seemed somehow life defining. The joy in their reunion telegraphed, "You are part of me, and I've been incomplete while we were apart." The bond looked capable of setting them both aflame. It was the purest manifestation of friendship I'd ever witnessed, without a whiff of the eroticism that we often assume is necessary for the deepest kinship.

The two of them beheld only each other as friends and relatives swirled around them, leaving them largely alone. They would throw their arms around each other, then pull back a bit and just look at one another with delight and wonder that they truly were *here, together, finally*. They took turns kissing each other on the cheek or holding the other's face between eager hands. And then they'd hug again.

I couldn't look away from the intimacy; maybe I should have, but I couldn't.

I wanted what they had so badly. I prayed for it while stifling cries that could have reached heaven itself, wherever that is, if I'd let them out. I felt crushing disappointment that I'd never looked at anyone nor been looked at that way and also a warm, bubbly delight at knowing that something like that was happening on planet Earth for somebody.

Tears were rolling down my face.

***

For a few years, like a moth drawn to flame, I frequently watched one of the last scenes in the movie *My Best Friend's Wedding*. I had learned over the years to pay attention to repetition and tears as clues to what God was trying to show me. This movie scene fit.

In the movie Julia Roberts plays a woman named Jules who has come to town to try to stop her best friend Michael from marrying the wrong girl, since she's now realized that she – always platonically connected – is the right one for him. The relationship between Jules and Michael is sweet, and yet the audience is willing for him to go off with his fiancée Kimmy – mostly because the plot is more nuanced than I'm describing. And that's what he ultimately does.

At the end of the movie the bridal couple goes off in their limousine with fireworks exploding, and then the camera fades back to lovely Jules sitting at a table alone as the reception winds down. Her cellphone, the size of a loaf of bread, rings. Jules answers and it's George, one of her other dear friends. George has secretly come to town to be there for her when her heart gets stomped, as he knew it would when Michael inevitably went off with Kimmy. Jules is relieved when he calls her to provide a lifeline out of her loneliness and doesn't know that George is actually across the room.

George starts mentioning things he would only know if he could actually see her. He says something about her lavender dress – she hadn't told him the color – and how her hair is swept up. He notes that she's sitting alone and not dancing, to which she replies cynically that dancing may happen in another 30 years or so. He muses that she hasn't touched the wedding cake in front of her. He teases that she's probably drumming her fingers on the white linen tablecloth the way she always does – which she is in fact doing. He says that she's probably looking at her nails and thinking she should have had a manicure; she is.

And the more George says, the more Jules feels seen and known and hopeful.

She jumps up and starts looking around. The crowd parts, and George swoops in for the rescue of his lonely friend. As the wedding band cranks up *I Say a Little Prayer*, George asks Jules, "Has God heard your little prayer? Will Cinderella dance again?"

He grabs her hand and leads her to the dance floor, acknowledging that he is in fact gay and therefore "Maybe there won't be marriage ... maybe there won't be sex ... but, by God, there'll be dancing."

I practically dissolved into a puddle on the floor every time I watched that scene as I did again writing about it because I myself so wanted – and want – to be seen and known and rescued that way.

I melt in the arms of a God who invites me to dance when I feel invisible, inhibited, passed over or alone.

Who finds me delightful just as I am – erratic and imperfect.

And sees the glory of who I could become.

I used to think healing was for others – you know, the screwed up people. And then I rushed to be first in line.

One night I just wanted to get out of the cold winter weather. My children were at youth group at our church, and going home and back would have been a hassle, so I decided to wait for them inside the nearby chapel where there happened to be a healing service going on.

Mind you, *I* did not need healing. Healing was for people who didn't have the package of a life I did. But the building was warm, so I figured I'd just sit way in the back for the hour, mind my own business, and read a novel while those weaker people worked out their problems with God. When youth group was over I'd go back into the cold night, scoop up my children, and return to our cocoon.

I'd been a Christian for a long time at that point. I'd put a lot of effort and white knuckling into trying to do faith *right*. I even read the Bible somewhat regularly. But I surely didn't *need* God the way some of these people looked like they did.

In fact if the truth was told, I thought God needed *me*, good little foot soldier that I was, always at the ready to talk about my cancer.

As I settled in to the pew that night, for some reason I decided to read the Bible there in the rack instead of the novel I'd brought. And my eyes immediately fell on this verse: "Call to me and I will answer you and tell you great and unsearchable things you do not know." There it was in the book of Jeremiah, chapter 33, verse three.

It might as well have been written in neon. It seemed like some sort of announcement: "There is more to life than you know; you can find out about it if you want to; God will talk back to you if you call out to him!" This was unheard of to me at age 40 even though I'd been in church since I was born and had been trying to be a Super Christian since I'd been *born again* after the shoplifting debacle.

My finger traced over the passage a time or two until a preacher interrupted my reverie. He didn't know me but he was describing my life. As I remember it, he was standing at the end of my row pointing at me, but since I've never seen a preacher do that – and I've seen my share of preachers – I imagine he was actually up front in the pulpit where he was supposed to be.

He talked about emotional distress as if it were normal, and he talked about relief as if it were possible.

He named what I'd theretofore only felt as a lump in my throat when I let myself admit feeling anything. He said that I couldn't breathe for trying to be perfect, that I lived in fear of screwing up and always felt that the other shoe was about to drop, and that I was going through the motions instead of living.

He insisted that I felt lonely, undefended, alien, orphaned and widowed, not to mention wretched, poor, naked, pitiful and blind.

And that some days I felt fine, if a bit flat.

And every day I made sure others didn't know how I felt.

And I was exhausted.

That's what he said. Or at least that's what I heard.

The omniscient preacher said that when we leave our places of oppression, our versions of Egypt if you will, we might as well go all the way to the Promised Land.

That sermon rattled my world badly – or rattled it well, depending on how you look at it – because I realized, as scales of denial fell from my eyes, that I really *was* in pain and that my life *did* feel broken. And that I *was* faking it most of the time.

Somehow everything I'd ever known consciously (that my life was objectively quite good) and much of what I knew subconsciously but couldn't yet admit (that life scared me and that I was hiding from it in an imposing fortress that I didn't want to be in anymore) coalesced around that preacher's message. I would never be the same.

If life can be divided into before and after, that was the

moment when the truth set me free – or at least that process began.

The fireproof life of denial didn't suit me anymore. If I'd consciously thought of it at all, it had seemed appealing, like the only option even. And now it didn't.

Then (get this!) the preacher said that if we wanted to we could go to the front of the sanctuary and people would pray for us. If we did that, he insisted gently, something powerful would happen: we would find God's comfort, and life would start to get better.

And in the very same instant that I felt sorry for any of the losers in the room who would believe that, much less go up there and trust strangers and act all vulnerable, I found myself rushing to be first in line.

I found myself kneeling in front of two church ladies. And the next thing I knew my hands were stretched out holding theirs, and they were praying for me. I don't even remember them asking me why I wanted prayer. It's possible that I produced some totally articulate string of words that explained how, although I thought my life was pretty darn good by anyone's standards, I nevertheless wanted – much of the time – to crawl into a hole and disappear. Maybe I went on to say that I couldn't quite figure out why, but the preacher's explanation of pain and longing for more had touched something subliminal in me so here I was. But I don't remember saying anything.

And in a few short and sweet words, one of those church ladies told me in no uncertain terms that I was in a lot of emotional pain, that it would be relieved, and that it was going to be lifted not just so I could feel better but so that I would be equipped for loving other people. She insisted that I had some sort of *calling* ahead.

I knew with absolute certainty that that was a true pronouncement from a deep place in the universe and that the rest of my life had just been shown to me. So I more or less skipped back to my seat, knowing, if only imperceptibly, that I was getting ready to road trip on out of the limbo I was living in to some great destination as yet unimagined, someplace I hadn't known existed until right then.

I was a bit stunned and even more pleased because I'd just been shown my current location, spiritually speaking. And everybody knows that all our journeys start in the here and now. Technically we don't have to tell God where we are; being omniscient and all, he knows. But sometimes it's important for us to name our starting point for ourselves. And I'd just done that.

I don't remember much else about that night. The ride home probably involved some fun conversation about a round of the Chubby Bunny marshmallow-eating game that my daughters had played at youth group or something, but we drove home and life went on.

***

Life went on. Of course it did because here I am telling the story almost 15 years later. But life as I'd known it did not in fact go on. Ever so gently, my new life began.

During a gnarly decade that followed, two years of which I've already admitted were mostly spent lying on my living room floor, God apparently sat down in his spare time and made a list of everything in my life that I clung to the way a monkey hoards a bunch of bananas. He targeted all those things I wanted so badly that I'd bite anybody who tried to take them away – perfect relationships, safety, guarantees, no conflict, and a reputation for omnicompetence as a start.

God then wrestled with me over each of those items until I collapsed in a heap or walked off with a limp like Jacob in Genesis, who wrestled with him too.

It was a slow, painful process, and for a long time I thought maybe all the feeling and hurting and aching and hungering and thirsting were worse than the denial and the dull, subconscious ache I'd felt before. It was a bit like getting that mastectomy for a disease I couldn't even feel.

I kept telling God he could have access to my whole life (as if he doesn't anyway). And I kept going, seeing just enough breadcrumbs on the trail in front of me to give me hope.

In fact I'd say I was brave. And tenacious beyond what I knew I had in me up to that point in my life.

I began to read the Bible more, and I found Hosea 2:14, "Therefore I am now going to allure her; I will lead her into the wilderness and speak tenderly to her." That's what was happening – a desert experience with a kind guide.

Around that time I also read in Isaiah 58:11, "The Lord will guide you always; he will satisfy your needs in a sun-scorched land and will strengthen your frame. You will be like a well-watered garden, like a spring whose waters never fail."

In the wilderness-wandering days I occasionally pictured myself becoming a garden, all dewy and verdant, alive and colorful, full of zinnias and ranunculi and Gerbera daisies and all the flowers I love. Maybe people would eventually want to stop by this pretty spot.

But not right away, apparently.

When I was in the midst of that season of life, a friend of mine said, "Don't worry! You're on your way to being a profuse garden full of flowers. But I have to admit that right now you look like a churned-up plot of dirt with weeds and worms showing."

Thanks. I guess.

It was hard to believe that all the struggles would end well because I'd always assumed – to the degree that I gave it any thought at all – that being healed and set free would, well, feel better.

It didn't for a long time.

A sort of call and response pattern began although I can't say that my calls to God were always conscious. Years later I read about an autistic 12-year-old boy and his father who got separated from one another in the ocean far away from their storm-tossed boat. As they drifted further and further apart, each treading water in the jellyfish-infested sea, their only connection was a call and response where the father would shout, "To infinity…" and the boy, an avid fan of Buzz Lightyear in the *Toy Story* movies, would reply "and beyond!" It kept them focused and alive until they were rescued 14 hours later.

That was how it was with God and me. I'd ask him pretty often if we were still moving the right way, maybe even "to infinity." Then I'd sense his answer: "And beyond."

Over time I started moving from complacent choices and the default roles I'd inhabited to experiencing and admitting deep longings that felt like they would kill me if they couldn't be satisfied – like the longing for love stirred up at the airport.

New parts of me came to life too. I felt like I was being rebuilt and strengthened from the inside out.

How could God tend to me so personally, what with keeping the planets spinning and the grass growing? Yet he did.

And does.

And will.

It turns out God's methods aren't one size fits all. He orchestrates personal, though sometimes socially awkward, interactions just for me.

If you've never been in a church service where they *pass the peace*, here's how it works: the pastor says, "Peace be with you," and then the congregation says, "and also with you." Then everybody moves around – a little or a lot depending on the church's traditions and people's comfort levels – and shakes hands, saying "peace" or just "hello" if they prefer.

It's not supposed to be something with a lot of follow-up. In fact that would probably be stalking. So I wasn't all that excited to start sensing that I should call a guy with whom I'd just passed the peace. I couldn't stop thinking about him as I was driving home from church. I just knew he was discouraged although I didn't really know how I knew. I'd shaken his hand about five or six weeks in a row including that day. He seemed nice, no sweaty palms or anything noteworthy. But I didn't know him.

I did sense, in an I-think-God's-talking-to-me way, that I should call him and check on him. I decided this was problematic on many levels: my husband might think it was strange for me to call a single guy I didn't know, I didn't have his phone number or even know his last name for sure, and I mostly just didn't want to do it because it was socially mortifying.

I started with the husband conversation; *he* thought I

should do it if *I* thought I should do it. I couldn't get off the hook with that one.

Then the guy's last name popped into my head after all, and I quickly thought of a person who would have his phone number.

I couldn't get out of this except to just choose to ignore it, but the idea was hammering pretty insistently on the inside of my brain like a little mad elf with a pickaxe.

So I got his phone number surprisingly easily, dialed the number, called this virtual stranger, and tried to explain my identity ("I've sat near you these last few weeks at church, the one with three children and the curly-haired husband, you know?"). He did know.

Then I got to the point, saying something like "You seemed discouraged today, and I wanted to just check in and see if you're okay."

And I was met with silence.

As I contemplated hanging up and switching my membership to another church and my address to another planet, he finally spoke.

His voice was halting as he said something like "I'm a preacher's kid, and I haven't been in church for years. A few weeks ago I started going to your church, but it didn't seem like it was really doing much for me. I didn't even know if anyone had noticed me, and one reason I was there was to connect with some people. I said sort of a prayer this morning, and I told God that if he didn't send me a sign that someone had noticed me, I wasn't going back. And, um, now you're calling me."

Typing this so many years later still makes me want to cry. We sat on the phone together, pretty much strangers, in the intimacy of stunned silence. I think I spoke first and the gist of what I said was, "Wow, God must actually be real."

I was left with dumbstruck wonder. How could it be that God was present and kind and speaking to each of us personally?

I know God's voice better now, and more times than not I say yes to whatever offbeat instructions he gives.

That habit started with passing the peace with the pastor's son.

***

Another time the call came to me. I was cooking for a party. My landline rang, and the screen projected the name of an elderly acquaintance. I knew her husband had died recently and I knew, as did much of America, that one of her family members had recently been convicted of a crime and was in prison indefinitely. I felt curious about why she was calling me, and I picked up. She had no idea that she'd dialed a wrong number, and she asked for someone who doesn't live at my house.

I said "She doesn't live here; this is Cary Umhau," to which she replied, "I know you. How'd I get you on the phone?"

I said, "I have no idea, but I want to tell you how sorry I am to hear about your husband's death, and I can only imagine what a horrific year you've had."

In a shaky voice, the normally cheerful lady asked, "Where are you?"

Not sure where she was going with this line of questioning, I told her what part of town I live in and that I was home, and she replied, "Oh, well I'm trying to find my friend because there's a storm coming, and I'm scared."

I couldn't imagine that she'd find me comforting since she had a particular friend in mind, and she and I barely knew each other, but I asked if I could do anything for her or if she needed me to come over, to which she politely replied, "Oh no, thank you."

I heard an insistent urging from the Holy Spirit, that voice I've since learned, through interactions like this, to associate with unsettling but ultimately thrilling requests. I realized I should offer to pray for her. I wanted to scream, "No!" thinking it would perhaps be one of the freakier things

I'd ever done (up to that point; this stuff is normal now for me). But I gagged out the words, "Do you ... want ... me to ... say a ... prayer for you on the phone?" to which she replied, "Oh that would be lovely, really nice actually."

And it *was* lovely. For me at least.

I used to live a normal, average (if a bit legalistic) Christian life. Now I'm not sure what normal is.

God is absolutely wild. Bizarre. Enigmatic. In addition to *holy, perfect,* and *magnificent.*

Some days I just can't wait to get up in the morning and see what will happen. And plenty of days I want to sleep forever and avoid the whole painful world – except that God often will surprise me on those days too so I might as well haul myself out of bed and open my eyes.

A couple of years ago, I was walking around my neighborhood and approached a bush that I'd passed many times. Hundreds of birds congregate in this one scruffy bush at an intersection near a traffic circle by my house. As I passed them, I prayed the most ludicrous prayer, "Lord, I want to be so close to you that birds will feel comfortable landing on my head."

As those words crossed the membrane of my spirit, if there is such a locality, I simultaneously thought, "Wow, cool prayer. Where'd that come from?" and "Why in the world did I pray that? I certainly don't want a bird on my head. I don't even like birds that much, not up close anyway."

Yet the more I thought about it, the more I knew I certainly *would* want to be the sort of person that birds liked even if I didn't want them to land on me. I mean, who wouldn't want birds to like you? It's so St. Francis and all, sort of groovy to imagine walking down the street with birds on your robes. Birds would be drawn to vestments tied with a rope far more than to my twenty-first century wardrobe, wouldn't they?

This whole thought took place over 30 seconds at the most. It was just a weird fleeting impression and also an actual prayer that I knew had come from somewhere deep within me or even outside of me but not from *me*, the everyday me that wants to be regular and liked, thought of as good but maybe not quite remarkable enough to have to do anything about it, the me that wants to fit in enough that I wouldn't probably invite birds to ride around on my head.

I dismissed the thought and walked on.

About three or four days later, I was heading into a nearby pharmacy. I ran into a friend on the sidewalk outside and stopped to talk. A few minutes into our conversation, I felt something on the back of my head. I reached up to brush it away, asking my friend, "What's in my hair?"

She said, "It's a bird."

"Weird," I said, annoyed by the interruption to our little catch-up.

At that point, my friend said, "There's the bird," and pointed to a little sparrow that was now standing between us on the sidewalk, nowhere near a tree, totally out of place, just standing and staring at me. The little fellow stood there several minutes. He had an amazing ability to hold a gaze.

My friend said, "I don't like birds, and this one is acting weird, so I'm going to leave before it dies or something."

Assuming for some bizarre reason that this bird had lost its ability to fly, I decided I'd better go into the store and ask a stock clerk for a box with which to transfer the bird somewhere – where? – so it wouldn't get trampled or struck by a car in this busy intersection.

I went in, asked for and received an empty receptacle, and headed back outside with it. Only as I slipped back onto the sidewalk through the automatic glass door did I realize that that was *my* bird, sent to land on my head in response to the inadvertent prayer several days before.

The bird had come to fulfill his little errand that meant who knows what. Now he was gone, nowhere to be seen. He hadn't waited for a ride in my box, which I tossed into a trashcan nearby.

I wandered home, scratching my head right where the bird had landed moments before.

***

Not too long after that I was on a sidewalk downtown

talking to a couple of friends. A woman approached, looking a bit disheveled and slightly wild-eyed, and I guessed she might ask me for some money. We made eye contact as I said a silent prayer for how to engage her.

She walked up to me, laid her head on my shoulder, and just rested it there. I cupped her chin in my hand and held her head for a minute or so, actually probably no more than 20 seconds although it felt much longer. The intimate exchange also felt oddly ordinary.

And then she asked me for money for diapers, and it didn't seem right to give her money, so I didn't.

She stomped off.

So much for our kumbaya moment.

A fireproof life helped me avoid inklings of pain, others' or my own. Now I believe we've got to be (and get to be) each other's balm.

I got to know a woman in the community who was in her twenties, was from a prominent local family, and struggled valiantly with depression and anorexia. Some days she was affable and other days agitated and fragile. I befriended her and would often ask how she was doing and what was going on in her life and family, just the usual neighborly interactions.

As time went on, she began to spill more of her story to me, admitting her pain and the weight of being unable to get well. Her confidences made me feel indispensible and important at first, and that sensation is my version of crack cocaine.

But if the truth is told, which it will be here, she quickly overwhelmed me. Her illness and pain scared me. I felt more and more impotent every time I encountered her sunken face, stooping shoulders, and shrinking frame. And I soon wished I'd never been friendly.

One night she showed up uninvited at my house during a dinner party. Through the dining room window I saw her approaching my back door, and my heart sank. I wondered how I would help her without ignoring my guests. I opened the back door to her plaintive glance and invited her into the kitchen where we stood awkwardly. She sensed that I wouldn't be able to give her my full attention; I sensed that I should invite her to join the party. I did. She didn't want to join us and soon went on her way. I could scarcely concentrate on the table prattle for wondering where she had gone alone in the dark. I agonized over whether she would take her own life that night; I wondered whether I should have insisted she stay. She was as proud a woman as I was, not prone to begging or showing up unbidden. And yet she had come, had not chosen to stay … and I'd been relieved.

I began to fear what would happen to her if (when) I couldn't meet her growing needs. I began to feel responsible to fix everything and to be there for her, although she was mercifully under the care of professionals. I resented my own role and wondered where her good friends, family and support network were.

I later realized that if someone is leaning on you that much then – well – you might just *be* her support system yourself.

So after the dinner party visit, I prayed that God would divest me of the duty I'd assumed.

And he did.

She had electroshock therapy and forgot about me.

When I ran into her, much healthier than before, she

seemed to think of me as simply someone to say hello to, a benign presence in her life. She remembered my name but she didn't seem to remember anymore that she'd poured out her heart and story to me many times. Those memories were gone.

I felt a brief glimmer of regret that all the energy and angst I'd poured into our friendship were gone in a poof, that I'd never get credit for any of my sacrifice, and that she clearly wouldn't be including a chapter about my devotion in her memoir.

Ambivalent as I was about being let off the hook, I could hardly go chasing after her, begging her to remember that I had mattered.

God really doesn't expect us to save the world. Sometimes, though, he'll give us a front row seat for some pretty wild rescues.

**

Another time my friend Joey and I drove a very drunk woman around town as we looked for her home. I don't think she ever knew she was with us, though her friend, to whom we ultimately relinquished her, might or might not have shared the story when she sobered up. I've always wondered.

We had found her down on hands and knees crying in the

bushes outside Joey's downtown apartment, and we told her we'd walk her home. She didn't remember where she lived – or much else. She careened closer and closer to the busy street as we discussed all this.

We asked her to retrieve her wallet from her purse and show us the address on her driver's license. She did, with some difficulty, and we then decided that the only logical thing to do was to put her in my car and take her home, relatively far away. We hoped against hope that she didn't resist or coat the interior of my beloved car with vomit.

Joey told her he was going to use her phone and call her friends. He tried a few people before he found one who both cared and could easily help, though we'd have to wait half an hour or so for her to get off work and help our passenger get into her building. Apparently her driver's license was not current and to get her to her current apartment we needed to drive south on the same road we'd just taken north.

We found the right building and began to wait for the friend to arrive. In the meantime our drunken cargo began sobering up but not enough that she would have been safe to get out of the car and be left on her own.

I found myself holding her head, stroking her hair, comforting her, silently praying for her while she told us stories of an old boyfriend and insisted that she was a slut.

When her friend came, she helped her out of the car. We

exchanged a few words and then slipped back into the traffic.

When I told my husband the tale later that night, he tried to convince me that we would have been liable if this woman had passed out or died in my car, unable as Joey and I were to prove that she had willingly gotten in, which she certainly had not been sober enough to do.

He reminded me that I had no idea what to do in medical emergencies.

He was right on all fronts. Probably even that we'd sort of kidnapped her.

All I can say is that it seemed right to do what we did.

And she didn't die.

And, certainly less important but still a major bonus, she didn't even vomit.

I sure do think of her every time I pass that building she lives in.

I hope you're okay, Nicole.

Poverty used to be an abstract issue. Now I have friends who are poor.

Once I was meeting Bill, a pastor friend of mine, at a coffee shop for breakfast. This was a regular occurrence for us, but it had been far too long and I felt starved for the camaraderie I anticipated. As I backed my car into a parking space nearby, I became aware of a mentally ill man on the sidewalk. I didn't see him directly; it was more like I felt his presence, ranting and weaving as he was.

I said a silent prayer that I could avoid him.

With more of a thought bubble than a transcript, I sensed God saying, "How about you just take life as it comes and not go out of your way to avoid my people, *people I love* by the way?"

So I tentatively exited my car, paid the meter, and then just tried to scoot across the area I needed to traverse to get to the breakfast spot. Which of course led me smack dab into the weaving fellow I'd seen. He wasted no time in asking me if I would buy him a cup of coffee. Three dollars honestly seemed like a meager price to pay to avoid a Gordian knot of an encounter with someone erratic. I started to reach into my wallet. Charles, whose name I didn't know yet of course, said, "Oh no. I want to have coffee *with* you. Can we go somewhere together?"

Crap. Not what I planned; not what I wanted. But since God and I had already been discussing Charles, at least in the abstract, I was fairly well prepped to say "sure." So I did.

Of course it helped that Bill was not only already in the coffee shop waiting for me but is also male, which made me feel safer. Charles and I entered. I introduced them, mouthing "Just go with it" to Bill as Charles and I sat down. We all began talking and decided what to order. Charles only wanted coffee, which was served with animal crackers on the plate. As he nibbled on a giraffe Charles morphed into a scared 10-year-old. He briefly became quite focused and lucid and confided that his mother was sick and he was scared. We tried to comfort Charles.

He then started slipping away again. First he simply stopped responding to anything; then he mumbled "thanks" and headed back out into the mean streets.

***

In another conversation, Bill told me that his church, called St. Brendan's in the City, was trying to take seriously a passage in scripture. It was Isaiah 58:6-12, and it sounded strangely familiar. He read it to me:

> Is not this the kind of fasting I have chosen: to loose the chains of injustice and untie the cords of the yoke, to set the oppressed free and break every yoke? Is it not

to share your food with the hungry and to provide the poor wanderer with shelter, when you see the naked, to clothe them, and not to turn away from your own flesh and blood? Then your light will break forth like the dawn, and your healing will quickly appear; then your righteousness will go before you, and the glory of the Lord will be your rear guard. Then you will call, and the Lord will answer; you will cry for help, and he will say: Here am I.

If you do away with the yoke of oppression, with the pointing finger and malicious talk, and if you spend yourselves on behalf of the hungry and satisfy the needs of the oppressed, then your light will rise in the darkness, and your night will become like the noonday. *The Lord will guide you always; he will satisfy your needs in a sun-scorched land and will strengthen your frame. You will be like a well-watered garden, like a spring whose waters never fail.* Your people will rebuild the ancient ruins and will raise up the age-old foundations; you will be called Repairer of Broken Walls, Restorer of Streets with Dwellings [italics mine].

The part about *Repairer of Broken Walls, Restorer of Streets with Dwellings* was inspiring, and I knew that Bill and his church were trying to bring some love to a tough neighborhood. I loved it when life and the Bible matched up.

Yet I started feeling a little guilty because I'd long claimed for myself verse 11, the part where it says, "The Lord will guide you always; he will satisfy your needs in a sun-scorched land and will strengthen your frame. You will be like a well-watered garden, like a spring whose waters never fail." In retrospect I realized I had thought I'd get to be a well-watered garden just because I was trying hard or I was special or because I'd spent so much time being worm- and weed-filled and surely enough was enough.

Yet now I saw that there was a *context* to these verses and that the promises were for those who spent themselves on behalf of the poor.

That wasn't exactly me.

I felt squirrelly about not having thought about that before. I also wondered if I really would "have healing and have my light break forth and my darkness shine like noonday and be joyful and have the glory of the Lord as my rear guard" and all those things if I started doing things for the poor. I didn't even know what all of that *was*, but it sounded so much better than staying all guarded and fireproof and safe.

I was feeling stirrings way down in my soul or somewhere, rumblings that made me want to keep going further and further, deeper and deeper into whatever God offered.

Yet I didn't want to *use* the poor and homeless as my escape mechanism. They had in many cases ended up homeless because of already being used for other people's purposes. I didn't want to compound that.

It was definitely something to think about.

And besides, I didn't know any poor people. So I could hardly spend myself on behalf of them.

Around the same time as the conversation with Bill I read these words from Mother Teresa: "The trouble is that rich people, well-to-do people, very often don't really know who the poor are; and that is why we can forgive them, for knowledge can only lead to love, and love to service. And so, if they are not touched by them, it's because they do not know them." I felt nauseous even as I wrote it in my journal.

Bill said I would find Jesus among the poor. That made no sense since I thought Jesus hung out only in church. But after a while I started just vaguely wanting to go to St. Brendan's, which met in a men's homeless shelter, the Central Union Mission, here in D.C.

I went, and I've never been the same again.

I felt scared when I first pressed tentatively on the cheap plastic doorbell and entered through the heavy glass doors. I didn't know what to say to the guys standing around or working at the welcome desk. I can barely conjure up memories of my initial fear because it's one of my favorite places now.

Jesus really is there, present amidst the hard stories and the bunk beds. It was a relief to begin to worship with homeless men who admitted pain and struggle, both of which are hard to hide there in a shelter. One night during church we were talking about good work being redemptive, and we broke up into little groups to talk details. A doctor spoke up; I said some *blah blah blah* about trying to write good stories. Then a homeless man in my group said, "I work for the National Park Service. I clean toilets in the picnic shelters and park facilities. And I can tell you that if someone visits the bathroom before I do my work and then after, they will tell you that cleaning up shit is redemptive work."

I was hooked. Enough of my posturing and self-importance. I realized I'd come home somehow.

***

One warm night a year or so later my husband and I waited on the sidewalk to go into a new restaurant on opening night. For a cover charge of 20 dollars, we'd have unlimited samples of the offerings at this new gourmet taqueria. As we waited in the throngs Ronald, a homeless friend from the Mission, walked by. I called out to him.

When he stopped to talk, I told him about the exciting party we were all waiting in line for. He lit up, asking us, "Is it free?"

"No," I said.

We talked a minute more and he soon wandered on.

Only later did it hit me that I didn't want to be at parties that Ronald couldn't go to.

And it hit me that I hadn't even thought of asking him to join me.

Life is too much sometimes and I can understand why people would rather *eat, drink, and be merry* than enter into brutal stories, their own and others. Yet Jesus is all over those stories.

If ordinary loves and losses can bend and break us, how do we bear the weight of the truly traumatic stories that some have lived and that are out there for the hearing if we're willing to listen?

How do we not run into the streets screaming, *"Stop all this pain!"* when we are privileged – as I have been – to hear stories of true anguish?

How do we begin to comprehend and contain all that results from our own missteps and from others' failure to love as we try to wing our way into the sometimes-cruel world?

For one season I sat in a windowless basement room and heard the stories of 25 people who had gotten clean through an addictions program at Samaritan Inns in D.C. The goal was to produce a booklet celebrating recovery success stories during their 25-year history. I was simply the editor, the one permitted to call forth the stories.

Much more than that happened.

One woman told me her story over several grueling hours. She ended our time together by saying that she wanted to call her sponsor from Alcoholics Anonymous to announce that she'd done the thing they'd both always wanted her to do: tell her story – out loud to another person.

As I looked into the brave face of that petite, 50-something grandmother, I saw her as the little girl who had been helpless when a stepfather had held her brothers upside down over an open stovetop flame. I saw a taxi-cab hitting her, and I pictured her mother suing and winning a settlement, telling her that she had money coming her way but then blowing the money on heroin to use with her brother and – worst of all, somehow – mocking her for caring.

I saw all of that in the woman jubilating over the fact that that story and those memories would not define her anymore and would no longer be kept in the dark. In fact healing was already bursting forth, the truth setting her alight right there as we spoke. I saw her spark and flame up, unstoppable and free.

***

I met a man who had been to the morgue to identify a girlfriend who'd died, a prostitute who was tagged with a *Jane Doe* label on her toe. He told me of screaming out, "She is *not* Jane Doe. Let me tell you who she is and where she came from. I *love* her."

***

I heard the story of a woman whose mother put her and her siblings on a mattress and lit it on fire, trying to burn them to death to get the attention of their father, who wouldn't give her a ride to visit a new paramour.

And I heard the postscript that this woman now visits that mother in Florida regularly – not exactly a holiday but nevertheless a journey she chooses, a peace offering that bears witness to the reality of forgiveness more powerfully than any sermon I've ever heard.

***

At a time when I was contemplating life's mysteries and coming to terms with my own fireproof tendencies, I encountered a man at Samaritan Inns who had his own fire story. He had been trapped in a basement during a serious electrical fire about 20 years before. In spite of the haze of intoxication and the temptation to give up and die, he had somehow known that God was calling him to fight his way up the stairs towards life. He ended up with third degree burns on 80 percent of his body, was in a coma for two weeks, had 23 skin grafts, and spent many months in the hospital.

Still largely covered in scar tissue, he radiates something holy and gentle. To hear him tell it, that demeanor came from years of regular, cruel taunting as he rode the buses and subways of our city with bandages covering everything but the orifices on his face as his burns healed. He carried a Bible in his lap to remind him not to react to people's jeers with anything but patient love.

Of course these are their stories and not mine. Yet my story now includes the hours spent with these and other courageous people who have suffered far beyond anything that I have known.

For reasons I can't fathom, they entrusted the tales to me, the woman who used to avoid everybody's pain.

I used to think, at least subconsciously, that being white made me superior. Now I realize I've got a lot to learn.

I was walking in what we have of a Chinatown in D.C. one night. I'd had dinner with a couple of friends, and I was heading back to my car a few blocks away. I passed through a thicket of people, tourists mixed with locals, professional folks heading out for 14-dollar cocktails, and others who would likely sleep on the streets that night. I heard a voice behind me demand, "Give me a dollar."

I turned, smiling, and said, "No." The young, well-dressed, black teenager insisted, "Then give me some change." Again I said, "No."

He barked, "Why won't you get me something to eat?"

Though the crowds were thinning in the evening darkness I made a split-second decision that, rather than turning around and walking back to a more populated area, I'd continue on down the sidewalk side by side with my conversation partner. This decision coincided with a silent prayer for knowing how to react to him, even how to love him.

I joked, "Why won't you get *me* something to eat? How do you know I'm not more hungry than you are?"

I'd felt peaceful up to this point, but his tone unnerved me a bit as he barked, "You're scared of me."

I answered, "Why would I be scared of you?" trying to sound upbeat.

"Because I'm *black*," he said.

"Hey, that's not fair," I reeled a bit, still hopeful. "Do you not like *me* just because I'm white?"

"That's right. I hate *all* white people. I hate *you*."

At that point, I stuck out my hand and said, "How do you know we wouldn't like each other if we had a conversation? I'm Cary."

To which he replied, "Get the fuck out of my neighborhood." Which I swiftly did.

But not before my heart was broken a little bit.

***

I was born in 1960 in the heyday of the Civil Rights era, yet as a teenager I didn't know that there was a racial problem in Atlanta or anywhere else for that matter. I just knew that on a hot day there was no way I was going to cool off at the integrated pool.

Nor would I be wearing the pants that Ray, a boy in my high school, had worn on his very own beautiful, black body. The wool U.S. Navy trousers, with a front, drop-down panel that fastened with anchor buttons, were the snazziest pants I'd seen on a civilian. I told Ray I'd long admired them. In an act of generosity, he gave me his beloved pants. It just didn't seem like an option to wear them and I never did.

＊

On my first day at the big public high school after several years in a homogeneous private school, I met a teacher who looked at the attendance roll and said, "Oh, I see where you live. They don't let black men like me on your street unless we're hired to cut the grass. Your people would probably throw bones at me."

My eyes opened instantly to the river of black help, theretofore invisible to me, that flooded my neighborhood each morning and rushed out again each evening when they'd finished baking cakes, mowing yards, and putting babies to bed.

＊

One of those black workers changed my diapers and made my dinner. She wasn't warm and fuzzy, but Mattie loved me well. She worked as a maid for our family and we loved each other with a bond that would have been more complicated between two adults. I was eight months old when she came to work for us in 1961. Mattie kept the job until my parents left town 27 years later. In her funeral program many years later, her daughter listed my sister and me – by then grown – as Mattie's goddaughters. Yes, I guess that fit.

Mattie rode two buses each way to work for my parents – with childcare, laundry and the requisite frying of chicken in between. She saved the livers for me. She knew how best to discipline my sister and me and had permission to do it.

She was part of the family – the part that had to clean our toilets, accept our cast-off furniture and clothes with enthusiasm, and wear a uniform that she changed into and out of in a damp basement bathroom reserved just for her.

With my stubby fingers I often traced the dark, ashy scar where a bullet had entered her hand as she tried to flee a fight in her neighborhood. The bullet was still in there, and it made her seem exotic and heroic. I thought it also explained why her handwriting was almost illegible.

She accompanied us on summer trips to the beach when I was young. On her nights off my father would drive her to a seedy-looking cinderblock nightclub that catered to the black help at the resort. I can still recall watching her scurry through the entrance, the screen door flapping behind her, and wondering why she thought it would be more fun in there than with me.

Many other nights at the beach, she took care of my sister and me. One night she sang along to a recording of *Midnight*

Train to Georgia as we danced at a beach bonfire. I twirled around her with utter abandon, certain that she was as exhilarated to be with me as I was with her.

When I was 19 I met the man whom I would ultimately marry. He fell in love with me, he says, when he first watched Mattie and me teasing each other while she ironed the family's clothes. He beheld not my public face but my comfort place and saw something in me I didn't yet see in myself.

From the time I was small, Mattie and I played a card game called *Pittypat*. It never seemed to have the same rules twice, always changing in her favor. Since she was the only one who understood the game, I had to accept the discrepancies. That game came to be a symbol for me of everything that was unspoken and immovable between us.

After I moved away from home, I kept in touch with Mattie mostly by phone. In one of our last conversations before she became too sick to talk, I said, "Mattie, can you explain *Pittypat* to me again?" I asked the question almost every time we talked; it had become something of a joke between us.

She sighed loudly and said, "Cary, there *are* rules for *Pittypat*. You just don't understand them."

For a long time, my prayers weren't much deeper than "God bless you" after a sneeze. And years later I'm still just a preschooler in the school of prayer.

I'd assumed praying was like going up to an information desk where one asks a direct question and gets a straight answer. I thought it was like a Magic 8 toy that I used to have, where you'd shake this black orb filled with soupy liquid until a little triangle appeared with an answer to your question – "Yes definitely," "My reply is no," or "Very doubtful." To be fair, it sometimes said, "Reply hazy try again."

For so long knowing Jesus was mostly about keeping my reservation for heaven current, the one I got when I prayed the *sinner's prayer* after my kleptomania ran smack into the middle-aged Sears store detective in the cheap suit back in 1973.

Instead I've discovered that prayer is more like conversation, a posture of openness. I used to seek pat answers and think there were formulas. I've come to see that every last object, moment, thought, and experience has meaning and might even be a delivery vehicle for something God wants to say.

And he speaks with love.

Always with love.

***

The first time I drove my son to camp in rural Pennsylvania, on the way there we passed a mailbox that had a sign on it: *Prayer Requests Taken.* It sat out in the middle of a big gravel parking lot in front of a nondescript, prefab church building, the sort of place that just as easily could have been an upholstery shop. I decided I'd scrawl a prayer on something and shove it in the slot upon my return trip. It became an annual habit for all the years my son went to that camp.

Before the Pennsylvania trip each year, I labored over an enumeration of my deepest aches and longings, limiting myself to the top quarter or so of the "Could somebody please do something?" list lodged in my little aching heart and flitting around in my head. In the second year, I added, "You'll hear from me every August with an update. Thanks for praying."

And then after I dropped my son off and headed home alone I'd zoom into that parking lot and cram my prayer requests into the little opening in the mailbox. I'd then lay rubber out of the parking lot, hoping that no one saw me because spilling my guts into the Pennsylvania Christians' mailbox was fine, but having them know who I was wasn't. Yet when I'd feel alone, as inevitably I did even with a semi-decent support system developing, I'd think of the little prayer team that would – I assumed – sit in metal folding chairs in a circle, hang their heads in solidarity as they pored over my scribbled prayers, and urge God to help me, heal me, and honor their prayers on my behalf.

And I'd feel less alone because of those praying Pennsylvanians.

Because I *was* less alone.

***

One of the great gifts of my small church is a young girl with whom I sat in worship most weeks before she moved away, breaking my heart a little. We're both energetic and would tend to do some serious swaying and twirling when we sang together. Being a child she had, not surprisingly, a simple, childlike faith.

We have teams at church that are available to pray with anyone who needs prayer. Occasionally a line forms. One night I was waiting for a turn to pray with one of the teams when my young friend approached me. She asked, "What's wrong? Why do you need prayer?"

I answered, sparing details in deference to her age, saying something vague about having some hard decisions to make.

She said, "You don't need to wait for the team. I'll pray for you." She took my hands and prayed out loud for me. As she walked away, I thought, "That was nice; now I'll wait for the prayer team so I can get real prayer."

Then I was appalled.

And went back to my seat expectantly.

**

A tree taught me that if we believe enough to pray, we have to keep believing long enough to act. A huge Dutch Elm in my yard, pride of the neighborhood, was sick or dying or so a visiting arborist told me when he happened to be a guest at my house. He couldn't help but comment on what – to his trained eye – was a tree emergency.

We dutifully called a tree specialist to come out and cut it down.

A short time later, I was passing the tree and felt a strong urge to lay my hands on it and pray for its healing. (That's weird; not normal. Don't think I don't know that.)

I put both hands on the tree, leaning in all close like, well, a tree-hugger. And I prayed, fervently, eyes scrunched; I asked God to heal my tree. I knew he could; I even thought he would.

I was with some friends soon after that, and we were praying together about whatever was on each of our minds. If

I'd thought about it, I might have censored this odd prayer, but I started praying for the tree with them.

Time passed, I more or less forgot about the prayers, and the tree men I'd scheduled earlier came out on their appointed day.

I was in my second floor office looking down on their work, and I could see the inside of the tree as soon as they made a major cut. And it looked like one perfect tree, not a damaged, sick, dying thing. I felt nauseous, realizing at once that I'd *asked* God to heal it and even *believed* that he could, but hadn't *acted* on that by cancelling the tree surgery.

And now an apparently perfectly healed Dutch Elm was being destroyed.

It was too late to do anything. The tree was now a nude totem pole, poking up out of my yard.

Later in the day I dared tell a neighbor about my prayer … and lack of faith. She stared at me dumbfounded and then said that the tree surgeons had told her that they didn't know why they were removing a healthy tree but that "orders were orders."

She mentioned her grandson, partially deaf, and asked me to pray for his hearing.

I did.

I don't think it helped.

Prayer was like talking to imaginary playmates until I learned to wrestle with God.

For years when I was upset, I treated every feeling as a major emergency. It was as if I'd notice a warning light on Zippy the Wonder Car's dashboard and, rather than making a mental note to pull over at the next gas station, I'd simply crash into the guardrails in a misguided effort to deal with the problem immediately. That was my emotional modus operandi.

On a particular day a few years back, I had a problem. I have zero idea now what it was, and the details don't matter anyway because *it's always something* for us discontent humans, or for me anyway.

I felt sure that if I could just call a friend, then everything would be okay. She or he would say the right thing, comfort me, and my anxiety would dissipate in the magic of our connection. Deep down I realized that any one friend's counsel would leave me needing more and that I'd end up banging on every door and dialing the phone number of everybody I knew.

In the midst of my apprehension I heard a little voice in my head suggesting that I didn't need to call a friend; instead I should just pray. And I immediately got on my knees.

No, that's a lie.

I decided instead that the ideal solution would be to go to the drugstore and buy and eat a lot of chocolate.

In two seconds I knew that that too was an inadequate plan.

And then Psalm 16 popped out of my head, right where I'd put it. Being a rule-following, legalistic sort of girl during those fireproof years, I'd been memorizing scripture somewhat regularly, a habit that served me well and helped me learn that it actually does have power.

I started sort of whining and talking all at once, using this psalm as counterpoint to my ramblings. I'd go back and forth in my head between what I was really feeling and what the psalm said was reality. I confess that I had this conversation in a moving vehicle, that there were not a few tears involved, and that I don't know where I drove in the 20 minutes that passed.

I'll let you in on my conversation, the best I remember it:

God, help. Help, help, help, help. Now.

Okay, your word says, **"Keep me safe, O God, for in you I take refuge."**

I'm not safe; how can you say that, God? I'm paralyzed and shaky.

"I said to the Lord, 'You are my LORD; apart from you I have no good thing.'"

83

I don't feel that way; I wonder if you're even good. If I'm honest, I want everything else more than I want you today. You're actually barely on my list.

"As for the saints who are in the land; they are the glorious ones in whom is all my delight."

Yes, God, I do like your people ... where are they all right now by the way? Why do I always feel so alone?

"The sorrows of those will increase who run after other gods."

Yep, I'm running after friends and food like usual.

"I will not take up their names on my lips nor pour out their libations of blood."

I don't want to obsess over something besides you; help me stop.

"Lord you have assigned my portion and my cup; you have made my lot secure."

I have to admit that in spite of my current problem, my life is pretty sweet. I'm not starving in a refugee camp; I live in freedom and safety. And beyond that, I have a good life ... even if I can't always feel it. I'll admit that. Grudgingly.

"The boundary lines have fallen for me in pleasant places."

Okay, I do acknowledge that. To not do that would be really bratty because I do have everything I need – and more. Even though I'm upset, this is all objectively true.

"Surely I have a delightful inheritance."

I'm trying to remember, God, that the life I have with you – on my worst days – trumps everything else in my life including these current problems. I know that you delight in me, that you look at me and love me, and you don't hold it against me that I'm having a rough time claiming all your promises and experiencing joy.

Honestly the thrill of life with you isn't floating my boat right now, but I will acknowledge that sometimes it does.

"I will praise the Lord who counsels me."

Who am I that you would talk to me personally? Is it really okay to rant and argue with you? You're not going to strike me dead, are you?

"Even at night my heart instructs me."

I realize I'm calming down a little, like I do after my husband comforts me when I wake him up to say I've had a nightmare.

"I have set the Lord always before me."

Well no, I haven't. Sorry I forget so often.

"Because he is at my right hand, I will not be shaken."

Without you I'm kind of antsy and broken; with you I do feel steadier.

"Therefore my heart is glad and my tongue rejoices. My body also will rest secure."

God, I know my emotions will come around; my courage will come back. I'll calm down. My equilibrium isn't gone forever. And I'll see my problem in perspective.

"You will not abandon me to the grave; nor will you let your Holy One see decay."

I believe Jesus' resurrection happened and that it applies to me. Pick me up from my own ash heap.

"Lord, you have made known to me the path of life."

I want to be on that trajectory where dead things come back to life; I'm desperate for it in fact.

"You fill me with joy in your presence, with eternal pleasures at your right hand."

I'm trying to remember to stick close. Help me. Thanks. Amen!

And with that "Amen!" I rolled into the driveway, wrung out though peaceful and with my issue settled. I'd moved – as the psalmist describes – from being a "brute beast" to being a "weaned child," something in me moving from *chaotic* to *settled*, from *crazed* to *content*.

Dan Allender, one of my favorite authors, wrote that "prayer is wrestling with God until we surrender to his goodness."[1]

I was waving my white flag.

* * *

I used to think that prayer should have a lot of *thee* and *thou*, but now sometimes I just groan or shrug my shoulders. In the years I spent lying on my living room floor staring at the fireplace full of ashes, I'd say to God, charred and incinerated as I felt, "You'll have to take my posture as a prayer. It's all I've got. I'm vaguely willing for you to come and get me up and do something with my life. Do it or not; I don't much care."

I was unable to forgive myself for deep relational longings that I'd deemed bad and now see as so, so good, evidence of hunger that, if I don't fill it with cheap substitutes, ultimately leads me to consume more of God.

"Ashes to ashes and dust to dust" was my cynical mantra as I lay on the floor waiting to live again; I don't recommend that as a focus or practice. Not because God won't respond (he did; he will) but because it's a giant waste of time and life to remain indoors in prisons of our own construction when we are invited out into the vast, endlessly fascinating world, which so much needs our attention.

There's a scene in the movie *Monty Python and the Holy Grail* where Prince Herbert is in a turret with the King of Swamp Castle, who stands by the window, gesturing beyond it, and says to him, "One day, lad, all this will be yours."

Prince Herbert, unable to see or imagine all that lies beyond the window and focusing only on what's right before him, replies, "What, the curtains?"

For a good long time, I was a "What, the curtains?" kind of gal when in fact I had a kingdom waiting. It was enough to crash on the floor and let God fight for me, eventually come and get me up, and orient me until I could see outside the window. And then push me gently out into the wider world, a phoenix slowly emerging from the ashes.

And sometimes now I stretch out on that same floor in worship.

I used to pull out a platitude or a Bible verse whenever I was forced to look at pain. Now I sense God inviting me to just *be* with hurting neighbors.

Tuesdays are my regular night for serving dinner at the Central Union Mission, where I first went to check out St. Brendan's and stayed.

My short frame hidden behind the steam trays, I'm simply a smiling white face with a mop of gray hair amidst the dozens of homeless men, mostly black, who file by hoping that we'll have something to offer besides the usual canned green beans with the meat and starch.

On a particular night, one man in the endlessly snaking dinner line caught my attention. I could feel his anger even before it was his turn to approach the food window. I summoned up a silent prayer, asking God how to meet his icy glare in our upcoming encounter over the rice and gravy.

As he stepped in front of me, I said rather haltingly, "Have you had a rough day?" Even as it came out of my mouth, I knew it sounded inane and condescending, hardly a logical or inviting conversational gambit for a seething stranger.

He looked at me with what felt like disdain and said, "No, not particularly. What I'm having is a shitty *life*. Here I stand in this line to get food, and there *you* stand on the other side of this counter with a perfect life, heading into – I'm sure – a 'happy holiday' (his dark, muscular arms punching the space between us with air quotes). That's what *I'm* thinking."

I inhaled and prayed wordlessly, wondering what response would come out of my sucker-punched little self. Unexpected tears began to escape my eyes, which soon stung with mascara as I said, "You're right. I have absolutely no idea how to make sense of the fact that I'm on this side of the counter and you're on that side. But yes, it's shitty."

He laughed almost gently, his wrath deflating a bit as he took his food from me, wandered out to look for a seat among the other men – none of whom looked too excited to welcome him – and began eating.

From time to time, he'd look up at me and smile almost imperceptibly as if he were thinking, "What the hell just happened? *That* wasn't what I expected."

It wasn't what *I* expected either.

***

Sometimes all we have are our tears – and our questions.

I don't understand why I get to live in a neighborhood where we won't let kids play in the cul-de-sacs after dark or consume drinks with Aspartame, while kids across town walk to school hungry and without gloves. Why don't I do something to alleviate the worries of their mothers, who are much like me … though typically a bit darker-skinned? Why don't I rant, stomp, and protest?

Why do I drive by drug deals going down in squalid alleys, singing *Daydream Believer* in my clean little paid-for car?

On the other hand, what would I do if I stopped? What makes me think I could help the situations that break my heart? Who am I to approach those who suffer with my glib answers? Why would I have anything to offer a hurting world?

As I write, multiple friends have terminally ill parents, and others ache with infertility. Friends have been sexually abused, don't have consistent places to sleep at night, deal with raging addictions, or go through the motions in empty marriages.

I know people who spend their days managing more-than-adequate finances but feel trapped in lives that others would envy, and who live with a nagging sense that they're not *really* living. Still others have names that the public knows but hearts hidden from everyone, including, they admit, from themselves.

And plenty of others just can't find the joy that they think they're supposed to have as Christians.

Most of these people, if you asked them how they are, would say, "Fine." Don't believe it; most of us aren't "fine."

Nowhere close. Not personally, not corporately.

How can we say we're fine when the planet is lurching and belching, leaning and toppling with weather weirdness, when wars rage, bullying kills, gun violence flares; in short, when evil tries to win out?

Some days I want to say, "Come Lord Jesus. And before lunch would be nice," but in the meantime we silly little people get to wake up every morning and join the fray. And do what we can in God's name and power.

The more I've discovered the depth of God's love for me, the more I've been able to let in the world's sorrows (and admit my own). Where else can they be contained except in hearts more and more enflamed by God's love? Anywhere else all that sadness would crush us.

As complicated as we tend to make it, it may be pretty simple. We receive as much of God's love as we're ready for, then show up when someone else needs it. And be honest.

We do everyone a service when we drop the posturing that keeps us from admitting, "Me too." We need to tell the truth, because isolated people become little lone sheep that can get picked off by wolves – all because they were convinced that they were the only ones who had shameful secrets, painful memories, or just normal messy lives.

Often when I fear or doubt or have a fall-apart moment, I

call my friend Richard, who came from Northern Ireland to be our pastor when Bill moved on. Invariably he says, "I don't know what you ought to do but I'm with you."

**

Recently I encountered a rather homely teenage girl with braces and freckles. She was part of a big, noisy church group that had come to town to serve the homeless at the Mission. They had matching, bright turquoise t-shirts that read, "We're white, we're right, and we're here to sing." No, actually they were probably only emblazoned with the name of their church. But I'm still prone to making judgments about people, and one of my latest targets has been groups of one-time visitors at the Mission – because I have a sick sort of pride in being a regular.

For some reason (likely the prompting of the Holy Spirit) I decided to stick around after my shift and hear them rehearse some songs that they'd be singing for the men in the shelter at the chapel service that night.

And a girl in the back row, singing along and doing sign language to the Casting Crowns song *Glorious Day*, soon transfixed me:

> *One day they led him up Calvary's mountain*
> *One day they nailed him to die on a tree*
> *Suffering anguish, despised and rejected*
> *Bearing our sins, my Redeemer is he.*

She didn't need attention; she wasn't playing to the crowd; she was worshipping a God she knows well.

The group's conductor motioned to this girl, clearly not one of the popular kids, to come up front. As she did she continued unashamedly worshipping, signing and gently swaying as she sang with a purity of focus on God – at an age where peer pressure is everything.

And all at once I was awash with the sense that beyond my own dark judgments, I am loved as immensely as she is.

I felt tears roll down my cheeks, tears that were united with her in worship as I sang along,

> *Living he loved me*
> *Dying he saved me*
> *Buried, he carried my sins far away*
> *Rising he justified freely forever*
> *One day he's coming, oh glorious day*
> *Oh glorious day.*

I used to wear flame-resistant pajamas. I was shocked to find I wanted to shed those itchy garments for something more organic: street clothes of love.

Nobody could have convinced me, the woman who was secretly afraid of life and most people, that I would in fact come to see every last person I meet as a potential friend.

I want to be open to the stranger encounters that I happen upon. Recently a certain Greg and I held each other's gaze for a while outside the Farragut North subway stop as he played his trombone. I silently sang, "From the halls of Montezuma, to the shores of Tripoli," some modicum of inhibition keeping me from breaking out dancing with passersby in that rush hour crowd.

When I realized I was running late, Greg and I shook hands. He said, "I hope I see you again."

I hope so too.

***

Soon after that I met a woman named Rachel on the sidewalk. She said, "Don't let my wheelchair and all this homeless-person stuff distract you from knowing that God is working mightily in my life."

"He's working in mine too," I confided. "In fact I'm heading to breakfast with my friend Scott to tell him a God story."

As she reached out and pulled me to her in an embrace, we smiled at the tears forming in each other's eyes, and I remembered my hopeful, silent prayer in Dulles Airport way back when.

Yes, love has found me.

**

The Bible says that God puts the lonely in families. For the most fortunate, they begin with our biological families and they explode from there. These multi-racial, multi-ethnic, intergenerational affiliations are laboratories in which we can lean into the truth of who we are – flawed and fickle and also glorious beyond our own imagining.

For a while I worried that the further I followed God, the less company I'd have. Most people want to keep some inhibitions and normalcy, and I've stopped caring so much. That's a little lonely at times. Yet I also feel delightfully connected to the whole human race, aflame with love for people without needing them so desperately like I used to.

There are people, good ones, who choose to keep going down Jesus' narrow path, who keep surrendering. I want to keep pace with them. I've come to have the coolest group of friends anybody's ever had. (Imagine! I'm the woman who, years ago, told someone that I had 225 friends I felt responsible to keep up with regularly yet only felt close to two of them.)

My friends and I from tiny little St. Brendan's church, so insignificant in the eyes of this city or the world, are setting banquet tables in parks normally given over to drug deals and eating homemade pie with the strangers we meet there. We call them *Flash Tables*; they are collective acts of love that we imagine Jesus might have done, living parables.

We've met eager, earnest tourists and hurting, lonely locals.

We've met gang members who checked us out from afar, then settled in and hung out with us, sharing stories and doing cartwheels in the grass. One of them shared a passage from his favorite book, *How to Win Friends and Influence People*. Another said to the rest of his posse, "Hey, we have food stamps. We could feed people ourselves in this park."

We've consoled a man just thrown out by an abusive lover and ended up celebrating his art opening at a swanky hotel a few weeks later.

We wanted to restore joy to a derelict corner that used to be known for music and hired a drummer who got us all dancing. Later we learned it was the same corner he'd slept on when he was homeless.

We've tucked a fleece blanket around a shivering mentally ill woman at the table, transferring her drink from a gold goblet to a blue one when we discovered that blue is her favorite color because sometimes love demands that you wash an extra cup.

This melting pot of a city desperately needs people to serve and stir the soup. Or slice the pie. As does *your* city.

And – God help us – we want to be among the ones in D.C. who say yes as we set the table for an ever-evolving love fest.

First I thought Jesus was confined to stained glass windows, and then I thought he might only be hanging out with the poor. Now I see that he likes dancing.

I asked some friends for prayer about something thorny just recently. One of them swiftly had an image of Jesus under a disco ball inviting me to dance. I'm sure that sounds totally wacko, as it would have to me if I hadn't gotten used to God meeting me very personally in prayer.

In my mind I accepted the offer to dance and pictured myself being twirled all around, like Jesus and I were in a crazy jitterbug competition or something. Jesus was delighting in me. He was strong and swung me up overhead so that I was practically vertical with my feet pointing at the sky. He had sprung to more life than those generic Sunday school pictures ever depicted.

***

Jesus and I have done a lot of miles together at this point. When Zippy and I go on road trips he rides shotgun with me in the form of a charcoal sketch taped to the dashboard.

I'd first encountered laughing Jesus, the *real* Jesus, I believe, when I was praying with an older, wiser woman one time. She was counseling me through some hard times. I felt stuck, and she suggested prayer. She told me to picture myself when I was little and "to invite Jesus to come into the memory" of the gawky self I recalled and to show me how *he* saw me, how he sees me now.

I felt self-conscious, not the least bit hopeful, embarrassed, and unsure of why I should put myself – or the praying woman – through the humiliation of asking Jesus anything, much less begging him to do something that clearly he would not bother to do, distant and busy as he likely was.

I acquiesced though, and we closed our eyes and prayed. In my mind I could immediately see myself standing in the hallway of my childhood home, looking like I did in a photo from the time, a fair-skinned girl in a homemade white dress with red trim, sporting braces and stubby auburn pigtails.

At the sight of my girlhood self I resisted, even sort of waving my arms and turning up my nose as I pictured myself as quite awkward. After several minutes of my trying to avoid her, the young girl in my mind started doing a little wiggly dance, all happy and bouncy and pleased with herself. And when she looked up she – a young me, of course – saw Jesus there with her, laughing and smiling with his head thrown back, just enjoying her and delighting in what I call my Snoopy dance.

And it melted me.

I suddenly knew that Jesus liked me, likes me now. A lot. Before that I'd assumed he didn't like me if he even knew who I was. Now I was certain that he loved hanging out with me. And that he saw me as, frankly, a masterpiece.

Like you are.

When I returned to work after the weekend during which I'd first seen this laughing Jesus in prayer, I went into my colleague's office where I regularly was. There behind his desk, taped to the bookshelf, was a line drawing of Jesus with his head thrown back laughing.

It had never been there before, but there it was.

I was a little freaked out.

I made several copies of it, and that's how Jesus started riding shotgun with me, though theologically speaking I'm aware that *I'm* the passenger, not him.

Who wouldn't want to travel with a guy like that?

I hear Jesus' laughter often now. And I just keep thinking about that disco ball and dancing like Snoopy – privately and more and more frequently in public too – or driving like mad out on the open road talking to him about whatever comes to mind.

I know I am loved.

People tell you that you have to go to church to hear God; you can find him out on the open road too.

I've adored church since childhood because of the tenor's voices, the coffee hours, and the cinderblock hallways that somehow telegraph security and belonging.

But I haven't always heard God at church. There's a lot going on.

One of my friends, Laura, sometimes asks great but strange questions as if they are normal. The thing about great questions and the people who ask them is that they help you find out what you already know (I've added some for you in the back of the book). The first day I met her Laura said, "What does God use to get your attention?"

Before I knew what my answer would be, I immediately answered, "Birds and road trips."

Maybe you listen best sitting in an easy chair with some Vivaldi in the background or floating in the ocean with the sun brushing your cheeks. As I've said, I personally hear God best while driving fast, with my brain half-occupied by shifting gears.

So Laura's question got me dreaming about being out on the open road with only God, creating room to find answers to some big questions I was asking as my nest emptied and my first grandbaby was on the way. I started hearing that Dixie Chicks line, "It takes the shape of a place out west, but what it holds for her she hasn't yet guessed. She needs wide open spaces, room to make her big mistakes."

I had heard someone, probably author and activist Shane Claiborne, say something to the effect that a normal day one place is front-page news in another and that some of us need to go to the *far country* and return with stories for those who can't or won't go. I liked the idea of going out in search of stories for others.

I decided I'd do a loop of the country alone, a rite of passage as I turned 50, and soon thereafter off I went.

One's brain generally finds handy diversions when out on the road. At a scenic overlook I stopped to relax for a few minutes and jumped rope for exercise until I read the signs nearby: UNSTABLE AREA and BE ON THE LOOKOUT FOR RATTLESNAKES.

I spent a little time contemplating whether people who commit crimes and are fleeing in getaway vehicles stop at scenic overlooks. I think so. Just because they did something bad doesn't mean that people aren't craving the natural beauty that's screaming out for their attention.

It made me think about how somebody who embezzled a lot of money from my family tithed on it, giving away a tenth of what she stole to her church. That's sweet in a twisted way.

If you're on the run or in a mess, I guess it still feels good to feast your eyes on grandeur or to do something good for somebody else, which makes me a bit more cautious about deciding that somebody (including me) is all bad or irredeemable.

It just ain't true. The story is not over yet.

Nobody's story is over.

As I drove, I thought up superlative awards like they give in high school – but not to me, I'll admit. Coeur d'Alene, Idaho won my prize for PRETTIEST PLACE AS SEEN FROM THE INTERSTATE. The Testicle Festival in Montana was TOURIST ATTRACTION LEAST LIKELY TO DRAW ME IN. MOST RANDOM, NON SEQUITUR REST AREA BATHROOM GRAFFITI was "Prince Charles *is* gay."

I spent some time worrying about whether I should have picked up a really woebegone guy back at the rest area in Minnesota, and then I spent more time feeling pretty sure that my husband would have said that I shouldn't. I moved on.

I paid a visit to Las Vegas to see old, retired signs at the Neon Museum's old neon boneyard, something I'd long wanted to feast my eyes on. I do adore neon.

And it was a kick to stand in front of the Fountains of Bellagio in Vegas, the sidewalks and sky ablaze with all the lights and drama and to see, far above it all, a full moon. Standing alone there in Vegas far from home, I felt deeply loved and right with the world as I shouted out loud to God (for in Vegas talking to oneself in public is just fine), "Your light trumps all."

Another day I saw some people having a car wash to pay for a baby's funeral and I thought I would just pull my car over right there and die of sorrow for all the tribulation in the world and all the tenderhearted, earnest things that people do to deal with it and to help each other out.

I wanted to revive that dead three-week-old and banish all the sadness of that family, that town, and the whole wide world. Instead I made a small donation because I already had a clean car and I didn't need a car wash. Besides, the line was really long.

Isn't life like that?

***

With all those wide-open spaces, God makes himself so obvious in purple and pink sunrises in North Dakota, in light filtering through pine trees on Whidbey Island, Washington, in the unexpected sight of Mt. Shasta around a bend in California, or in the white sands of New Mexico. We just have to go looking and keep our eyes peeled.

My involuntary reaction to all that beauty was an exclamation of "You have stinking got to be kidding me!" I found myself saying it over and over. It's as good a prayer as any.

All that splendor was just hanging around waiting for someone to come and see it.

My soul was coming alive more and more with each mile I drove. And then my mother left a voicemail for me when I was out of cellphone range one day, simply reading this poem by Rainer Maria Rilke.[2] I now had the words for what I had been experiencing:

> God speaks to each of us as he makes us,
> then walks with us silently out of the night.
>
> These are words we dimly hear:
>
> You, sent out beyond your recall,
> go to the limits of your longing.
> Embody me.
>
> Flare up like flame
> and make big shadows I can move in.
>
> Let everything happen to you: beauty and terror.
> Just keep going. No feeling is final.
> Don't let yourself lose me.
>
> Nearby is the country they call life.
> You will know it by its seriousness.
>
> Give me your hand.

As my son would say, "DAAAAMMMMNNNN!"

I used to believe life was black and white, either all good or all bad. Now I see that life has lots of *both/and*.

Since God called me forth from the fireproof hotel, I've never been myself again. Or perhaps that's when I began to be the *real me*, twirling around with flowers all over my body like I used to do as a teenager or rolling down hills with arms and legs akimbo, or road tripping around, open to meeting strangers, knowing that God's glorious people are everywhere.

It's possible that for a few minutes each week I may even be a version of the fully alive human being that Irenaeus talked about, one that glorifies God.

My life includes many of the things that I thought I'd die if I didn't have; in fact it always did. But those are the icing on the cake. It turns out that God himself is the treasure I was after – not perfect family and friends, my own omnicompetence, the good life as defined by Oprah or the internet, amazing adventures, or even the call to serve him.

Just God.

The *summum bonum*.

The be-all and end-all.

At some point in the difficult decade during which God

called and responded, comforted and shook me up, tore down the old, falsely-constructed me and built me back up stronger, things just began to be more good than bad. I gradually began to believe more than I didn't believe. I started seeing Jesus as intriguing, then compelling, and eventually as truly good news.

I came to the point where I wanted to scream from the rooftops – and fire escapes – that beyond all the talk, God really *is* present and more than a match for all that ails us. And that we can really love others, even the tricky ones, when we ask him to empower us.

The girl who used to avoid everybody now loves being in the thick of things with people. I want to be implicated. I want to belong. I want to be loved and to love well.

Of course the flip side of opening my heart to love is that there are even more ways for it to break as I let more people into my life and commit not to ignore or deny harm and pain. With infinitely more connection and community than I used to have, my florid imagination can envision even more horrors. I now see every squirrel as a threat, assuming they will become crazed at any moment and dive-bomb my grandchildren.

I remain inconsistent and goofy. At this late date I'm probably not going to become cool or quiet or give up my addiction to adrenaline or consistently remember to put mascara on both eyes.

Even after we're set free and transformed, we little human creatures are still often mean and messy, self-focused and myopic, prone to trying to make life work apart from God.

I continue to be a poster child for brokenness and vulnerability, although Sears has probably taken down my wanted poster by now and replaced it with a new generation of teenaged shoplifters' mugs.

My life is still a swirl of heartache and joy, pain and happiness. Within the span of a half hour I can sob over a newspaper story about a child killed by gunshot and then feel delight over a perfectly blazing fall leaf or the goodness of a neighbor who, yet again, patiently walks by my window holding hands with her long-demented husband.

**

I was on a walk on a perfect 68-degree day recently. The breeze was blowing and the trees were rustling. I was happy to be alive, which feels nice since it wasn't always the case. A song I'd never heard shuffled up on my iPod. It was the *Osanna* from Bach's *Mass in B Minor* and it positively soared, lifting me with it in worship as I walked around the neighborhood, not much caring how crazy I looked as I sang, swayed, and walked. I was enraptured by the music and how it kept time with the light filtering through the oscillating trees. I decided that I had to stop and just bask in all that sublimity.

And as I lowered myself down to the curb, I put my hand in a big pile of dog crap.

And I just laughed out loud because even in the most glorious of God-infused, God-given moments we still live in the real world.

Now and not yet. Both/and.

I can sit in that tension. Sometimes literally.

Oh yes, I long lived fireproof. Now I even ask God for *more* fire. And sometimes I have to look away when his fiery face is more than this flawed human can behold. But then I look again.

Wheeling, West Virginia is not so far away from my home in D.C. On a recent road trip I suggested to my husband and son that we stop by there so I could show them the crazy building they'd heard so much about, the God-sent metaphor that had taught me so much. They obliged and we took the exit.

I cheered out loud when I saw that the Rogers Fireproof Hotel was not as I had left it. *It's being renovated; it too is coming back to life.* The boards on the windows were gone and I could finally see into the lobby and the bar that I'd long envisaged.

I'd been on a long, arduous quest and had circled back to an important place I'd passed along the way only to be reminded that I'm not the only one who's changed, who will. I'm not hogging anything. There isn't a finite supply of grace.

My two favorite men shared my glee and photographed me in front of that building, a reunion captured for posterity. We're planning to go back and spend the night when the renovation is complete. What a party we'll have there at the Rogers Fireproof Hotel!

***

I recently saw a little girl, about seven, in an airport. She was waiting for someone's arrival with her grandmother, who was intent on stopping her from twirling in circles. The older woman barked at her over and over, "Stop that; you'll get dizzy."

I could hardly keep myself from screaming, "Grandma, what in the world is wrong with 'dizzy?' Do you want this poor child to spend her life in a straitjacket, stymied from twirling when someone she loves is on the way to see her? What's she saving herself for?"

Let's all be twirlers. Let's.

Dance music really is playing.

Jesus is beckoning us to join him under the disco ball. He's inviting us to dance in the streets of our cities with long-lost and newfound friends.

He wants to ride shotgun with us, his head thrown back in laughter, as we drive out into the spacious lives he's had planned for us all along.

Come on. Are you in?

It won't be the same without you.

To infinity and beyond.

AFTERWORD: SPACIOUS

Near the end of my wilderness decade I had the chance to create and launch SPACIOUS, an organization that subversively works to end loneliness and prejudice. We help people create and find the belonging and community we're all made for.

We've put on dozens of events in D.C., Baltimore, New York, and Los Angeles to connect folks with others through the arts, service, culture, and over meals. We've brought together people who might not normally have met – homeless friends hanging out with media personalities, tourists and gang members eating pie together, a six-year-old leading adult recess and showing the big folks how it's done.

We've consulted, spoken, and helped organizations and people, through customized offerings, to reimagine the dignity and worth of every God-created person.

We've fanned the flames of people's ideas and stories, offering a space where their gifts can be shared for the common good.

My SPACIOUS partners and I continue to ask God what it would look like to create a kingdom vision of community – and how we can help.

You can learn more, share what *you're* doing, and join in at www.spacious.org.

» Looking back at childhood, what are the scenes you recall in which you were most fully alive?

» What makes you feel fully alive or keeps you from feeling that way?

» Do you have a formula for the good life?

» What are the various cultures you inhabit and what does each expect of you?

» Fill in the blank: If I didn't have _____, I would just die.

» What has disrupted your perfect life, and what have you done with the disruption?

» Who is the *them* to your *us*? Do you know them by name?

» What makes a day good versus bad?

» What sorts of messages are being repeated in your life?

» What movie or book scene is your favorite and why?

» What brings you to tears?

» What is God like? How do you think he sees you? How do you know?

» Do you believe Jesus laughs? What makes him laugh?

» What do you believe God has promised you?

» How do you hear God best?

» What were you, uniquely you, born to say "Hell, yes!" and "Hell, no!" about, and are you doing those things?[3]

» What do you wish people knew about you? To whom do you want to risk telling it?

» Who needs you to show up, just as you are, today?

» Do you know how loved and adored and amazing you are?

Notes

1   Dr. Dan B. Allender, *To Be Told* (Colorado Springs, Colorado, Waterbrook Press, 2005), page 180

2   Rainer Maria Rilke, "Go to the Limits of Your Longing" in *Rilke's Book of Hours, Love Poems to God*, Anita Barrows and Joanna Macy, translators (New York, Riverhead Books, 1996), I 59

3   This idea comes from an article by author Dan Allender, *Getting Caught by Your Calling (http://bit.ly/RerAcd)*.

ACKNOWLEDGMENTS

I used to read other people's book acknowledgments and think, "You say it took a village; how hard can it be?" Yet another thing I thought I knew and didn't.

From way back, Lila Campbell led the way in teaching me to be big-hearted.

Mrs. Valentine let us do anything we wanted on Thursday nights for homework. SPACIOUS and other dreams were born back there in the fourth grade when I wrote a lot and had the kids in my class over for elaborate parties.

If there are grammar and punctuation mistakes in this book it's probably because I missed one of Bob Morrell's seventh grade English classes to go to the orthodontist. I should have skipped Math.

Chris Frost taught me that tears in public are a wondrous thing and that how we make somebody feel matters more than telling them what we think they need to know.

Weezie Thompson, Amy Hartman, Roberta Martin, and Sharon Gustafson, dear friends all, called me forth and also called forth a book. Often. As did my grandmother Anne Dodd.

Editing a book reminds us that we are far better with others than we are alone. These friends risked my defensiveness as they read and commented on various versions: John Gillis, Richard Treacy, Ron and Kathryn Ivey, Scott Borger, Mary Ann Calhoun, Sue Kranz, Nick Bian, Mary Silcox, Ryan Simpson, my children and husband, Elizabeth Boesen, Sharon Gustafson, Joey Katona, Roberta Martin, Allison Gaskins, Elizabeth Rice, Jacki Waring, Ryan Holladay, Becky Allender, Justin Noseworthy, and Dan McCarthy.

Others who've invested in the book include Deby Dearman, Penny Carothers, Brandon Andress, Tasha Kolar, Karina Saunders, Julie Wan, Kate Rehberg, Lisa Treacy, Sunita Groth, Rebecca King, Sarah Boone, Anne Cregger, Hayley Darden, Susan O'Banion, Don Miller, Laureen Naik, Rob Krech, Somer Salomon, Melissa Medley, Brandon Anderson, Lisa Shirk, Anne MacDonald, Lee Ferron, Amy Julia Becker, John Stiff, Cristina Liebolt and Susie Vernalis.

The good people of The Seattle School of Theology and Psychology (formerly Mars Hill Graduate School) and its Allender Center, individually and collectively, have sacrificed in ways I'll never know to bring life to me and many others. They do holy work.

Katie Chamberlin dug a hole and lowered me on a mat to Jesus when I didn't much think I wanted to go through the roof.

Joey Katona jumped off the pages of *People* magazine and into my life and left me shaking my head in wonder. He helped me see that I liked being on fire, even as he told me, appropriately, to get over myself.

Scott Borger conjured up a trombone and a tuba at 8 a.m. on the streets of D.C. to keep me going. His contributions to art and life are inestimable. .

Ben Kolesar is my co-worker in building arks and books. I love his powerful One Page Bible project; check it out at www.onepagebible.net. What a cliché to say that I couldn't have done this book without him – but I value the truth above everything. This book is almost as much Ben's as it is mine.

And reader, I acknowledge you. It's always about the one person in front of us, and here you are. May you hear God in your own native language and dare to follow him to greater depths of love.

Made in the USA
Middletown, DE
10 March 2015